ANN JAMIESON

FOR THE LOVE OF THE HORSE

VOLUME III

D0061535

*Until one has loved an animal, a part of one's soul
remains unawakened.*

Anatole France

Volume III Format and Design by
Elizabeth Vaculik

Cover Photo: Teddy and Karen O'Connor
competing at the Rolex Kentucky Three Day Event
Photo courtesy of: Diana De Rosa

Back Cover Photo: Jamaica, Chester Weber, and the rest of the team
competing at the World Equestrian Games in Aachen, Germany
Photo courtesy of: My Weber

CONTENTS

INTRODUCTION

Anyone who loves horses will appreciate this book. These are all true stories: stories about the bond between horses and humans. That bond is not particular to one breed or one discipline; it encompasses everyone who spends time in any way with these incredibly generous souls.

I wrote this book to celebrate that bond, to honor the horse. Horses bring so many gifts into our lives in so many ways.

This book is a thank you to my horses,
to horses everywhere.

Acknowledgements

I would like to thank all of the horses and their people whose stories are featured in this book. A special thank you to the superstars in the horse world who took time out of their crazy schedules to share with me about the horses that they love: Andreas Helgstrand, Matt Mills, Karen O'Connor, the Towell family, and Chester Weber.

Thank you to all the wonderful photographers who allowed me to use their pictures of these amazing horses.

Thank you to Hobbes for once again keeping me company through all hours, and always knowing which key to step on if I was unsure.

Thank you to all who asked for another volume!

Thank you to all my friends for their support and encouragement: particularly Roseanna DeMaria, for telling me I could do it when I doubted myself; and to Diana De Rosa for her generosity in allowing me the use of so many of her awesome photographs.

Thank you to Tucker for always reminding of all the ways horses hold special places in our hearts.

And a huge thank you to my team, Beth Vaculik and Natalia Zunino—you two are the best! You have helped make this book all that I wanted it to be.

DEDICATION

To Hobbes
My best buddy, my collaborator
A huge soul in a small package
Thank you!

love

⤳ Love Song

I was alone in the barn. Or so I thought. It was late at night; the other boarders had long since left and the staff had fed hours ago.

I had had a beautiful ride on the Rombout Hunt trails with Tucker, my stunning former racehorse. The sun had been setting as we returned home, casting an incredible pink glow across the landscape. Sunsets in that area were some of the most beautiful I had ever witnessed.

I had put Tucker's tack away and I was grooming him in his stall. His coat shimmered, dappled dark bay with chocolate and cinnamon highlights. And he was gorgeous. With the exquisite classic Thoroughbred head, long neck and perfectly angled shoulder, deep well sprung ribcage and strong rump, he looked every bit the racehorse he had once been.

However, his career now was as a show hunter and trail horse. He was amazing as a hunter, with a graceful, elegant stride and lightness that made him a joy both to watch and to ride. He jumped so easily and lightly that it all seemed effortless.

As a trail horse, well, he had his moments. Sometimes he was great, at other times he found mountain lions in every bush and rock.

As I brushed him, admiring his coat and build, and enjoying the nuzzles from his incredibly soft muzzle, I thought of how much I adored this horse. The more I thought about it, the more I realized it was true.

I'm not a singer, in fact, dogs howl and cats run under beds when I attempt a song. But hey, I was alone and overcome with emotion for my beautiful horse. I couldn't help it. "Wise men say," I began, "only fools rush in." I started low and tentative, but as Tucker looked at me quizzically my love for him overpowered my better judgment and I got louder and more passionate. Soon I was sure that I was Elvis reincarnated, belting out "I can't help falling in love with you."

I was almost through the song when I caught a movement out of the corner of my eye. I shut my mouth immediately and felt the burn moving up through my neck, spreading across my face until I was far brighter than the sunset I had just witnessed. It was Jose, coming out of a stall two doors down. The jar of poultice and Saran Wrap he carried let me know what he had been doing.

He looked at me, but didn't say a word. He simply smiled and continued on his way.

I only sing in the shower now.

⟿ Idis

Cherryl Mitchell was in the market for a Grand Prix horse. The horse she had had become too old for the physical demands of the top level of dressage. Hearing about a top contender in Canada, she and trainer Cathy Morelli traveled north to take a look at the horse.

Cherryl and Cathy both liked him. Idis had been a top European champion, with very expressive passages and piaffes. Cherryl had the 17.3 hand German warmblood vetted, and purchased him.

When he arrived at Cherryl's Richer Farm, Cherryl realized just what a wreck he was. Because of his enormous gifts, especially for piaffe and passage, Idis's former owners had unwittingly pushed the horse too far, too soon, leaving him anxious and stressed. The bundle of nerves was so anxious that Cherryl says, "Without an anchor, you weren't stopping him."

She decided to give Idis some down time: a chance to be a horse again. He was turned out in a paddock for six months to play and to relax.

Cherryl's student Helene Freixe is a novice, still uncomfortable around horses, especially big ones. However, she found herself "irresistibly and inexplicably drawn" to Idis despite his imposing size.

The first time Helene was introduced to the huge horse, Idis was eating his dinner. Cherryl and Helene were standing by his stall when Cherryl called him over to them.

Idis walked calmly to where they stood. It was Helene's first encounter with such a powerful (and top level) horse. She stood there, an impressed and intimidated beginner, staring at him.

Idis looked Helene over, smelled her hand thoroughly and, deciding that there was nothing there that required his attention, he slowly turned around and returned to his stall to finish eating.

Helene was instantly taken by his character and "aplomb." This was a horse she wanted to get to know. The following weeks, from the outside of his paddock, Helene commenced her "courting."

At first, she simply said "Hello." Next, she convinced Idis to follow her from one side of his paddock to the other. Helene continued to catch his interest with carrots and a few German sentences she had picked up.

One day, Idis stood quietly by the rail as she groomed and scratched his withers. She was quite amazed when he turned around, offering his opposite side.

Eventually, Helene gathered the courage to enter his paddock. The particularly merciless flies that weekend prompted her to volunteer to spray the big horse.

Idis was eating in his stall, which opened out to his paddock area. After fly spraying him from the paddock on the side nearest her, Helene had to move between the immense horse and the stall wall to complete the work. Not at all comfortable with the idea, she stood still for a moment, hesitating. Idis solved her problem by interrupting his meal and turning around. As soon as Helene's work was done, he simply turned back to resume his meal.

A few weeks later Helene entered his paddock to offer him some carrots. Idis happily chewed one, and tried to grab the second one. Helene "thought that this was a good opportunity to refine my budding 'leader' skills." She placed the second carrot behind her back, asking him to wait: "Sie Still." Idis stood quietly for a few seconds, then turned his back to her and headed for his stall.

Idis simply was not the type of horse to beg for a carrot. He had too much dignity for that. It was Helene who ended up doing the begging, but he had none of it. Finally, she dropped the carrot in his bucket and left, very disappointed.

In short order spending time with Idis in his paddock was no longer an intimidating prospect for Helene. Instead, "Stepping into his paddock was entering a magical world. I most often felt humbled before such a perceptive, intelligent being. His presence and awareness were remarkable, his gaze penetrating, his mind always at work."

Idis had arrived at Richer Farm wary of humans and what they might expect of him. Cherryl and Helene slowly and persistently broke down his barriers, to everyone's benefit.

After a few months of visiting him consistently on the weekend Helene sensed that he was beginning to open up to her. When he chose to let her in, she "felt a mix of awe and joy. I used to say that spending time with him was the equivalent of a deep massage."

The more time she spent with him, the more she became impressed by his independence and assured, almost introspective, demeanor. Idis always tried to understand, communicate, and make his own decisions.

For Helene's birthday, she asked for permission to take Idis to the large arena and "exercise" him.

It turned out to be one of the best birthdays ever. She says, "It was lovely seeing this imposing horse rolling in the sand and snorting with excitement like a young foal." With Cherryl's direction, Helene lunged Idis first at the trot and then at the canter. Although Helene was intimidated, she "was essentially in awe of such power and beauty of movement."

The day ended with an entertaining hosing session. Idis

managed to grab the end of the hose and it was Helene, rather than Idis, who got drenched.

Just as Idis learned to trust Helene, she, too, learned to trust him, realizing that he would not use his size to harm her. "His power was mixed with exquisite gentleness. He had a keen understanding of his size and power. The carefulness with which he moved around me always will astound me."

Helene was elated when one day she came to see Idis and he approached her with a spring in his walk, pointed ears, and a welcoming snort. She spent some time in his paddock...sitting under a tree, just hanging out, reveling in the joyful greeting she had received.

The previous weekend Helene had attended a clinic where a German rider had given her a couple of words and sounds used in Germany. *"Brav,"* she was told, is their endearing term equivalent to our "good boy."

"Brav," she told Idis. At the sound, Idis perked his head and came closer to Helene with a short snort. "This to me," says Helene, "was better than any prizes."

He also ate his carrots with particular excitement, snorting and stomping his foot with delight. As she was leaving the farm that day, yelling her usual "Goodbye, Idis!" the horse did something he had never done before: he stopped eating and stuck his head out of his stall with hay hanging from his mouth and an inquiring look. It was a lovely sight for Helene.

Helene and Idis only got to spend a short time together, yet their effect on each other was transformative. For the novice to the horse world, this "giving, exceptional horse and a gentle soul," gave her the experience of connection and "the rare magical bond that sometimes happens between horses and humans." Helene was honored.

To Idis, sharing a bond with this person who demanded nothing more than his company brought him back to the most essential part of the horse-human relationship and a well-deserved sense of peace.

(You can see Idis in "The Best Horse in Europe" which can be viewed on YouTube.)

ROCK STARS

⤳ THEODORE O'CONNOR

Capturing the heart and spirit of America, Theodore O'Connor's diminutive size and "can do" attitude inspired all who saw or heard of him. Besides attracting a following previously unseen in the world of eventing, the "Super Pony" became known in all equine circles and beyond, inspiring people to do their best and reach past perceived limitations. No one could watch Teddy compete without feeling uplifted.

Owned by the Theodore O'Connor Syndicate and ridden by Karen O'Connor, Teddy's accomplishments included a third in the CCI **** at Rolex Kentucky in 2007 (his first CCI **** event), team and individual gold at the Pan American Games in Rio de Janeiro, sixth at Rolex in 2008, and being short-listed for the 2008 Olympic Team.

Teddy was elected Horse of the Year in 2007. In addition, a new perpetual trophy was established in his name to honor top event ponies: "The Theodore O'Connor United States Eventing Association Pony of the Year" trophy. A new jump that will be built on the Rolex course in Teddy's honor is in the planning stages.

With such an astounding record and fan base, one might think Theodore O'Connor was born to greatness. No such luck. His breeder, Patricia Wynn Norman, says, "Of the four in his crop, he was the most awkward of the bunch. Physically, he was built like a sausage on legs; mentally, he was goofy, doofy, and shy."

In an amazing coincidence, he was also named Theodore O'Connor, not at the time of syndication as many believed, but from the time he was only a week old. The fiery redhead had managed to kick nearly everyone in the barn in just his first week, so he was named after tennis bad boy Jimmy Connors. The "O" was inserted just to connect the two names. Teddy's barn name remained "Connor" until Karen began referring to him as Teddy.

Teddy was lucky to be one of four babies because Wynn didn't have time to pay much attention to him. She had a dozen horses in total, many of them in full work, so Teddy ended up getting the time he needed to grow up. By the time he was the only one left unsold from his crop, he was mature enough to show Wynn he had traits worth developing.

Teddy's sire Witty Boy was a stakes-placed allowance winner, grandson of Bold Ruler, and one of six sons of the Maryland stallion Anticipating who stood at stud in the non-racing market. "Witty Boy" was his Jockey Club name but he was known around the barn as Theodore. Theodore produced major winners in hand in the midwest from his first crop. His brothers also produced show horses, and one, Anticipation, was a national caliber Regular Working Hunter, showing at Madison Square Garden and other prestigious locales.

Teddy's dam, Chelsea's Melody, was bred to be a broodmare. Her dam, Chelsea, is Wynn's foundation mare and as a result, Melody is half-sibling to countless successful hunter ponies, including a national champion. Melody is, Wynn says, "probably the most unique 13-hander you could meet. She is bizarrely hot, temperamental, and sometimes downright mean, especially toward other horses. She is phobic about having her legs touched—she'll allow it, but if you are too abrupt about doing so, she'll snatch her leg away so fast, she has a calcified bump on one hind leg from kicking herself so much as a baby."

Now 18 years old, Melody still snatches her leg away. She is so wired that Wynn taught her to piaffe in hand in a single day.

Wynn says that "Without a doubt, it is Melody who puts that 'desire to go clean' in the teddibabies."

The combination of a Thoroughbred sire with Melody resulted in Teddy's unique mixture of blood: 3/4 Thoroughbred, 1/8 Arab and 1/8 Shetland.

Wynn started Teddy as a show hunter, and then went on to compete him in the jumper divisions. When she moved to West Virginia and had 400 acres to ride on, she discovered how much he loved to run and jump. Wynn says, "You could feel Teddy's eagerness to see what was around the next turn in the trail and his glee in discovering a fallen tree to jump. He just ate up the countryside."

Taking Teddy's cue, Wynn's focus turned to eventing, and the pony competed through the Preliminary Level under Nicole Villers. Some of Teddy's events, right through Advanced, were about as promising as his childhood. In one YouTube video, Teddy makes a thoroughly undignified entrance, leaping into the dressage ring.

Christan Trainor continued Teddy's career, competing at Intermediate and then later on moving him up to Advanced and an eighth place finish at his first CIC. Needing some help with Teddy's flatwork, Christan got in touch with Karen O'Connor, introducing Karen and Teddy. Both Christan and the O'Connors were wintering in Ocala, Florida, so Christan asked Karen for some lessons.

As Karen explains, event horses tend to move up according to how well they are handling the cross-country phase. In many cases, their dressage education lags behind. It was difficult for Teddy to collect his canter; he didn't know how to sit. And his flying changes were explosive. Christan wanted help with these challenges.

When Karen first saw the pony, she could barely believe that Christan was doing Intermediate on a mount that small—

never mind planning on Advanced! Yet right away it was apparent to Karen how smart and powerful Teddy was.

Karen gave Christan a few lessons, working on developing his canter and smoothing out his explosive flying changes. During those lessons, Karen never saw Teddy jump. Later, when she first saw the pony jump, her reaction was, *"Wow!"*

After the winter, Karen and David left Florida to head home to Virginia. For a while, Teddy disappeared from their lives. Then, Karen heard from Wynn. Teddy was now about ten and Wynn had decided not to continue having him campaigned by Christan. After trying unsuccessfully to sell the pony, she wanted Karen's advice on what to do next. Unable to contact Karen by phone, Wynn sent a letter via an oversized, red-white-and-blue Priority Mail envelope to get Karen's attention.

Karen recommended that Wynn have Teddy campaigned by someone well-known so he would get noticed. When Wynn asked Karen who she thought could ride a pony like Teddy, Karen responded, "Well, I'll ride him for you!"

And that was that. Wynn says that, "Despite a fall at a fence at their first competition together, Karen never wavered from her commitment to Teddy."

Teddy had been turned out for several months prior to his arrival at the O'Connor's Stonehall Farm, and his part-Shetland heritage had come to the fore. Fat and unfit, the pony was in need of some serious conditioning. The initial plans for competition were scrapped, and Teddy was aimed at Radnor Hunt's two star event, as it would be easier to get him fit in time for that.

Karen discovered that Teddy rode like a much bigger horse than he appeared. His huge canter stride took her by surprise, and his athleticism was remarkable. He had so much power that the difficulty proved to be just what to do with it all. And his emotional fragility made him nervous, even of his own power.

When coach Mark Phillips first saw Teddy jump, Karen

suggested to Mark, "He has rocket fuel in him, doesn't he?"

"No," Mark responded. "He has a rocket in each leg."

Karen knew exactly what Teddy's potential was. Within three months from the time Wynn sent the Priority envelope, the pony was no longer for sale.

Karen credits Wynn for doing a great job with Teddy, and for allowing him the time he needed to mature. "She was very nice to give me complete care and custody of him with no questions asked. He was her family member, she loved him, and she just trusted him with me."

In no time Karen realized just how easily Teddy could manage an Intermediate course, and this encouraged her to move up to Advanced. When she did, she was amazed to discover that the more demanding level was just as easy for Teddy. So she moved him up to more difficult tracks, such as Jersey Fresh, a three-star event (where they placed 9th), and Fair Hill. Again, he continued to amaze her. Every task she asked of him, he accomplished easily and enthusiastically.

Teddy had also become a rock star, attracting dedicated fans that would travel hundreds of miles to cheer their favorite pony on at different events. The roar of "Go Teddy," followed Karen and "the pony" around every cross-country course.

He was surrounded by an adoring crowd at home as well. Teddy enjoyed a sweet relationship with David, who doted on the pony. Teddy's groom Max Corcoran and his vet Dr. Kent Allen were devoted to him. Teddy "needed the strength and love of those around him." Karen says, "He depended on his people to believe in him much more so than the average horse."

Teddy also enjoyed getting to know his fans. Pony clubbers who came to meet their hero mobbed him, and it was obvious just how much he loved being loved by the kids!

Teddy had now established himself as a three-star horse. The question in Karen's mind was, "Is he a four-star horse?" While she considered the question, she, David, and Wynn founded the Theodore O'Connor Syndicate, enabling the O'Connors and Wynn "to share Teddy's journey with a group of people who understand how special he is." Karen "looked forward to continuing his all-important education, so he can realize his potential and tower over those twice his size."

"Should we think Rolex with him?" Teddy's family wondered. It was a big decision for Teddy, and for Karen's career. The Super Pony's fans needed to be taken into consideration as well. Karen did not want to put Teddy in a position where he might fail, nor did his fans want to see him fail. Would Rolex be too much for Teddy?

Karen agonized over the decision, for, ultimately it was hers to make. Finally, she decided to go for it. She completely trusted Teddy and his superlative athletic ability, and knew that he completely trusted her as well. In fact, Karen said, "His trust in me went beyond what I thought was possible."

So, in April of 2007, Karen and Teddy headed to Kentucky. Although Karen had decided they would enter Rolex, she didn't start the course in a competitive fashion. Not wanting Teddy to make any mistakes or to shake his confidence, they embarked on the Rolex CCI**** course cautiously, slowly. Karen used her vast experience to give Teddy a ride that would make the difficult track as easy as possible for him. She had several horses in the field, but Teddy was the first to go: a good spot for them.

But half way through the course, Karen wanted to kick herself. Why on earth had she gone so slowly? They were about 30 seconds down on the clock, an eternity at the half-way mark. And Teddy was romping through the course with consummate ease. There was no need to be slow, to be cautious; this pony was eating it up!

Karen kicked him on, and was astounded at the response. Teddy accelerated like a rocket! She found herself sitting on a fresh new horse; she hadn't even begun to tap into his resources. The powerful acceleration shaved 15-20 seconds off of the time, and they finished the course easily, accompanied by the roar of an exhilarated crowd.

Karen's already tremendous respect for her Super Pony increased yet again. He'd made Rolex, the toughest course in America, look like a walk in the park. It was an incredible round, and a great ride for not only Karen and Teddy, but for everyone who witnessed it.

Spectators had crowded the entire course, roaring in approval, shouting the now familiar "Go Teddy, Go!"

The announcer, caught up in the excitement, was just as astounded as Karen and the crowd at the pony's achievement. Teddy, the announcer said, was "Absolutely flying!" and made the water complex "look easy!"

"This little pony," he continued, "he just grows as he goes along."

It was an improbable finish—the most unlikely pair in the field, the littlest horse (a pony!) ridden by the oldest rider. "Never in my wildest dreams," said Karen after her finish. "It's been like a fairy tale. I've never had more fun than I had this weekend with this pony. He feels like a giant out there."

They finished third with only 4.4 time faults, taking the coveted "Best Conditioned Horse Award."

Teddy's third-place finish in the event qualified him for the Pan American Games. Riding against horses with far more experience, Teddy and Karen went to Rio and brought home both individual and team gold medals. Again, Teddy proved what incredible heart and work ethic he had. The victory gallop brought smiles to all: Karen and her miniature mount were dwarfed by their much larger teammates.

In 2008, Teddy and Karen placed sixth at Rolex, earning

a spot on the short list for the Olympic Games.

Karen has had a lot of great horses in her life, but few have been as special, or had as much impact, as Teddy. Sometimes, Karen says, "You cross paths with something in your life that was just meant to be." Teddy came into her life at a time when they needed one another. He had the athletic ability and desire for greatness, but needed a rider who had the experience to guide his brilliance in the toughest competitions, and the tact to deal with his fragile emotions. (Heartbreakingly, it was this fragility that, in the end, proved his undoing.)

Karen, at 49, was questioning her future. "Where am I going? What should I be doing?" At the time, she didn't have any superstars at the top level in her string. Should she keep eventing at that level?

Bringing the two together brought out a sum larger than its parts and gave eventing, and the world, a luminous star to focus on and cheer for. Like the little engine that could, Teddy showed the world never to underestimate talent and heart because of size.

Teddy gained confidence from Karen's experience. He had all the ability in the world, but it made a lot more sense to him to do the job that he did with someone who had done it so many times. For Karen, who was questioning the direction her life should take, Teddy provided a direction, an answer.

Karen says, "He was one of the smartest, kindest, soundest horses I've ever worked with. He was so tough and stoic, a true athlete and a real gentleman who showed up for work every day." Teddy accumulated numerous accolades during his career, but Karen is particularly proud of his "Horse of the Year" win.

Theodore O'Connor was perhaps the only event horse who ever crossed the lines in the horse industry. People in all disciplines knew about Teddy; people who had nothing to do with horses knew about "the pony." He made The Washington Post several times. At a time when athletes are behaving badly, here was an athlete that had it all: integrity, honesty, ability. Teddy impacted anyone who saw, heard, or read about him. He gave people hope, inspired them to reach for their dreams no matter who they were, and to pay no heed to any so-called handicaps.

A freak accident ended the life of this small super hero. Teddy was being ridden when he spooked, bolted, and dumped his rider. In his panic he fell and slid into the side of the barn, lacerating his right hind leg beyond any chance of repair. Karen, David, and Wynn would have done anything for their friend, but there was nothing that could be done.

News of Teddy's death rocked the horse world and beyond. E-mails, flowers, and condolence cards flooded the O'Connor's farm. The USEF website put up a link where mourners could send their condolences to the O'Connors. So many e-mails (over 100,000) came in that they crashed the USEF website.

"He's terribly missed; he's in my mind every day," says Karen. "I miss the sweet pleasures of success with him, but the thing I miss the most is him."

Teddy's work on earth may have been fulfilled, but there are still more things for him to accomplish. As Karen says, Teddy left because "God has other things for him to do."

➵ Blue Hors Matine

The announcer at the World Equestrian Games declared, "It's not often that I am at a loss for words, but this is just one of those moments." Once he found the words, he expressed what the crowd was experiencing. "It is an absolute privilege to watch this horse. She is the sensation of these championships."

This horse was Blue Hors Matine, owned by Blue Hors Stables and ridden elegantly, and in absolute harmony, by Andreas Helgstrand. The nine-year-old mare, as the announcer said, was "absolutely dancing." He added "This horse just gives everything and seems to love every minute of it. This has just shot the competition into another gear."

As the freestyle progressed, the superlatives continued. "Absolutely unbelieveable! What a horse! What a performance! Absolutely brilliant! The crowd is joining in; they've never seen anything like it!"

The overflow crowd of 40,000 spectators packed in every conceivable corner had chills running down their spines, tears running down their faces. The brilliance, the harmony, the correctness and elegance of this horse and rider dancing to the music was absolutely breathtaking. The crowd was on its feet, it was perfect, perfect. Overcome with emotion, they couldn't stop cheering. Even when the test was over, they continued to clap in time with Matine's movement as she passaged down the centerline.

One of the most surprising things about one of the most

amazing rides in dressage history is that it almost didn't happen. When Matine was seven years old, Andreas came very, very close to selling her.

Matine came to Blue Hors when she was five, in April of 2002. Already, she was good. She won the Danish Young Horse Championships as a five and a six-year-old. She was very sensitive, yet easy to ride.

At seven, things changed. She got hot: very hot. She was so difficult and so wild at times that Andreas felt she should be sold.

Luckily for Andreas and for the world, it all changed when Matine turned eight. Once she began the demanding Grand Prix moves of passage and piaffe, she no longer had the energy to be wild. She was just too tired! As she became easier to ride, all the pieces started to fall into place and soon it became obvious just how incredible she was.

For Matine, piaffe and passage are not only easy but a lot of fun. Andreas is extremely humble, and is quick to give Matine all the credit. Of the brilliance and joy that we have all seen, he says, "That's her way. She has that power, that joy, and expression. It's natural for her."

Like a lot of great athletes, Matine is a bit opinionated. Working around her, she has the air of a princess. She doesn't care much for being tacked up. When her legs are being bandaged, she snaps them up as if to say "don't touch me!"

Despite Andreas' humility, anyone watching can see the incredible partnership he and Matine share and the brilliant job he does in allowing her joy and expression to shine through.

Andreas began riding when he was seven. His uncle has ponies and when he and his brother saw their cousins riding, they wanted to do it as well. There was just one problem: they kept falling off! Andreas' brother tired of hitting the ground and quit. Andreas was a bit fearful because of all the falls, yet stuck with it. (The rest, as they say, is history!)

Soon his father became involved as well and purchased a few horses. Andreas and his father were gone so much with the horses that his mother got lonely. She suggested they get their own farm.

The family purchased Soren Valentine in Aalborg, Denmark, where Andreas continued to ride and learn for the next six years. When he left his family's farm, he moved to Holland and worked for Ann Van Olst. This was followed by a short stint in Norway. In 2001 he got a phone call from Blue Hors Stud in Denmark. They wanted to know if he would like to ride for them. He would. Thus began Andreas' partnership with Matine and a terrific string of successes that included winning the Danish National Championships four years in a row (riding four different horses), silver and bronze medals at the 2006 World Equestrian Games, and a bronze team medal at the Beijing (Hong Kong) Olympics.

After the show stopping performance at the WEG, the rest of the world, those unlucky enough not to be in attendance the day of Matine's test, were quickly brought up to date by YouTube videos that circulated around the world. The sensation of the games was soon a global phenomenon. Many predicted World Cup and Olympic Gold.

A mishap at the Las Vegas World Cup in 2007, however, proved disastrous. Matine slipped while being unloaded from her van. She was lame, and to the immense disappointment of the crowd (many of whom had traveled to Las Vegas just to see her) had to be withdrawn. Although the injury seemed not to threaten her career at the time, she has not yet been sound enough to perform again.

Andreas has since left Blue Hors to form his own business, Helgstrand Dressage. The world may never get to see Andreas and Matine compete again. But, at least we all had the chance to witness a ride, a partnership, that transcends time and surpasses all we have seen before.

⎯⁀⊃ JAMAICA

It's a Cinderella story, through and through.

What is known of Jamaica's history begins in a Belgian slaughterhouse where the horse was destined for someone's dinner plate. Fate intervened in the form of a skin disease (probably ringworm), which saved him from slaughter. Fearing the infection would spread throughout the rest of his livestock, the butcher sold him for next to nothing.

Mark Wentein purchased the Hackney/Dutch warmblood cross to use in his carriage business, carting sightseers through the city of Bruges. Although Jamaica had lost a lot of hair, he was still a good-looking horse and was broke to drive.

Jamaica, opinionated from day one, passed on the tourist carriage option as well. An important requirement for these carriage horses is the ability to stand still, with no one at their heads. There is some down time between clients; in addition, the horses need to stand quietly while passengers climb on and off the carriage. Jamaica failed this test miserably. Standing still just was not in his vocabulary; he wanted to be on the move!

Jamaica's energy and athleticism led him to a new home with Valere Standaert, a combined driving competitor. The sport of combined driving (which consists of three phases, similar to eventing: dressage, marathon, and cones) demands bravery and a forward nature. The third option turned out to be the right option: Jamaica had found his future career.

Valere knew Chester Weber, an international caliber four-in-hand driver, and realized that Jamaica sported similar markings to Chester's horse, Hanzi. In driving, an important consideration is for the horses on a team to match. Size, color, build and markings all should be as similar as possible.

Chester happened to be in Germany at the time looking for horses, so Valere, thinking he might be interested, gave him a call.

"I have the perfect horse for you."

Chester listened, but he had heard it all before. Chester's horses are bays, around 16 hands. Some of the "perfect" horses he'd seen in the past stood 18 hands high or were chestnut or grey. Chester knew better than to get excited until he actually laid eyes on a particular horse.

Normally, the route between where Chester was in Germany and where Jamaica currently lived in Belgium would take about three to three and a half hours of travel. However, truckers were protesting high taxes, and they had blocked all of the major arteries. Chester, along with his friend Michael Freund, had to drive to Belgium using only back roads. The long, frustrating trip took over seven hours.

Chester nearly turned back several times. "Is this trip really worth it?" he asked himself repeatedly. He called Valere several times. "Is this horse really the right color? Is this horse really that good?" The answer was always yes.

When they finally reached the barn, an exhausted Chester wasn't in the most charitable of moods. He knew they had the long return trip ahead of them, and the horse had better be worth it.

He was. At first sight of Jamaica, Chester thought, "Wow!" And yes, the horse was the right size and the right color.

Inspecting Jamaica's conformation, Chester noted that the horse toed in. Still under the influence of the arduous trip, Chester wasn't sure he wanted to watch him go.

Luckily, Michael urged him on. "Oh come on, give him a chance," he told his friend.

Chester relented. Watching Jamaica go, he was relieved. The horse traveled straight, and had good gaits.

It was time to drive him.

Initially, things didn't go all that well. The horse was fresh and had his own ideas about how to do things. Chester wasn't sure Jamaica had the makings of a team player.

Michael, a knowledgeable and experienced horseman, came to the rescue by making some changes to Jamaica's bit and bridle. The changes resulted in a significant improvement. Driving Jamaica now, Chester became wildly impressed. He thought, "This horse is better than the one I have at home!" As he was thinking of just how good Jamaica was, Michael brought him up short.

"Chester, stop driving."

"What?" Chester said. He was having so much fun with Jamaica, why should he stop?

"Stop, now!"

Chester's respect for Michael made him listen and he and Jamaica pulled up. Only then did he realize that Valere was starting to get an idea of the horse's potential as well. If Chester didn't stop now, the price would go way up, or perhaps Jamaica wouldn't be for sale at all!

Chester asked for a brief trial period, which Valere agreed to. Chester looks for bravery, character, movement, and a ground-covering stride in his competitive partners. Jamaica filled the bill. In fact, Chester says, "His bravery is probably his best quality."

Jamaica was purchased and shipped to New York. From there he continued on to Toronto, where Chester was competing in the Royal Winter Fair.

In Toronto, Chester wanted to have some time to get to know his new horse, whom he planned to use as a spare, but the crowded venue offered little opportunity for schooling. He improvised, taking Jamaica out for a spin in the parking lot. Jamaica went so well Chester used him that evening. Jamaica has barely missed a show since.

The horse once thought to be nothing more than an item on the dinner menu has now racked up just about every four-in-hand award there is. He and Chester, along with the other members of Chester's team, have won the Four-in-Hand National Championship six years in a row. One of Chester's goals is to win it again in 2009, which would make him the first person in history to win the award seven times.

In 2008 Chester and his team won every selection trial in the United States, the German International Driving Derby at Riesenbeck, took third at Aachen, Germany (winning the dressage phase), and took a silver medal (the first individual medal for an American) at the World Championships in Beesd, The Netherlands. At Riesenbeck, their dressage score broke the world record. At Beesd, Chester and Jamaica then proceeded to break their own record!

Chester says he asks a hard question of his horses: "Are you good enough to win a medal?" The horses have to share that goal. Jamaica, without a doubt, does. He has competed in two World Equestrian Games and four World Championships, winning the dressage in two World Championships and placing second and third in the two others. Although Chester has a terrific team of horses, it is Jamaica who is his "Most Valuable Player."

In one YouTube video, Jamaica seems to be directing his equine team member, pushing the other horse to turn here, *now*, go *faster*, Come *on!* His drive and desire to win are unmistakable.

Jamaica plays two roles on the team. In the dressage phase, Jamaica serves in the wheel position, which requires a willing worker. In the marathon phase, Jamaica takes the left lead position: lead horses must be brave and forward. "Only the great ones," says Chester, "can fulfill dual roles like that."

Jamaica in no way takes after the laid back, no worries guy his name conjures up. Instead, Chester "has never had a horse with more spirit." In his stall Jamaica can resemble a Rottweiler defending its turf. He gets charged up at the beginning of a marathon. At the World Championships in Beesd, Jamaica, 17 at the time, had just completed the rigorous event and was brought out for the awards ceremony. He came out fresh and bucking.

At times, Chester's grooms tease him. "We have to give Jamaica more food; he's too quiet." Chester retorts, "Let him be too quiet!"

Jamaica has never fit into Chester's program. Instead, Chester had to figure out a way for Chester to fit into Jamaica's program. Chester likes to "think that working with Jamaica is like doing business with organized crime—you need patience and understanding with this horse because if you aren't flexible it won't go your way."

Although Jamaica works willingly with certain people, there are others that he "doesn't see any reason to be nice to." Despite all the attitude he may show in his stall, or with particular people, when his harness is on, Jamaica's ears are forward and he is always on his job.

Chester says that "a big part of me hopes he'll still be with me at the World Equestrian Games in 2010 in Kentucky." Chester's goals for that event are two gold medals. Jamaica, he says, is tough enough and strong enough to do it at 19; in fact, he has the character to be successful in his twenties.

Chester adds, "Maybe he'll be quiet by then. But I won't hold my breath."

There is one thing Jamaica has "no worries" about. His future. He has a forever home at the Weber family's Live Oak Stud in Ocala, Florida. "He has to be with me," Chester jokes. "Who else would put up with him?"

In 2008 Chester was named an Equestrian of Honor, winning the Becky Grand Hart Trophy from the USEF. Not only is

Chester a top competitor; he is a compassionate and generous human being as well. When his friend, eventer Darren Chiacchia, suffered a life-threatening brain injury after a terrifying cross-country fall, Chester pitched right in, managing Darren's farm, and overseeing lessons and sales. The fact that Chester was in the midst of preparing for National Championships didn't deter him from the formidable task one bit.

Jamaica was not about to be outdone. The former reject from a slaughterhouse achieved the highest honor of any horse in this country, joining the ranks of dressage star Brentina, Olympic gold medalist show jumping sensation Authentic, and eventing's superstar pony Theodore O'Connor. Chosen from horses of all breeds, and all disciplines, Jamaica was, in 2008, named United States Equestrian Federation Horse of the Year.

When Jamaica's win was announced at the USEF's annual meeting, the audience erupted in a standing ovation. Says Chester, "It's been a real honor to share this journey with an unbelievable horse."

⚮ Monday Morning

When his long, but not particularly illustrious racing career ended with a bowed tendon, Monday Morning was sent to the slaughterhouse. At least that was the plan. Two trucks pulled up to the barn Monday was housed in. One was headed to the killers. The other one was taking some mares that had been purchased as broodmares to their new home.

Monday got on the truck with the mares.

When Monday got off the truck at the new place, the owner looked at him and thought, "Well he's awful pretty, but he's not a mare." With his nearly black coat and beautiful eye, Monday was stunning. The mares moved into their new home. So did Monday.

Monday's bowed tendon made him dead lame. Luckily, because of his beauty and his sweetness, the woman decided to keep him. She rested him for a year to give the leg a chance to heal.

The time off worked. Monday came back sound and ready for a new career. When he started back in work, his owner discovered she had a horse with extraordinary talent. Although she realized she didn't have the money to bring him along and unleash his potential, she knew exactly who to call. She had heard about Andrew Lustig, a young trainer who worked with hunters and ponies. Taking a rescued off-the-track racehorse (Conversation Piece), Andrew had shown him to Horse of the Year honors in the hunters.

He was the man she wanted. With him, Monday would have a chance at greatness.

Monday's first brush with death was merely the start of a series of occurrences which would prove Monday catlike in the number of lives he seemed to have. Monday was shipped down to Jacksonville, Florida from New York in 1993, the year and the exact time of The Perfect Storm (The Storm of the Century.) The two horse trailer containing Monday, who was clipped and without a blanket, got stuck in a snowdrift on the highway. Fearing for his life, his owner took him off the trailer and they started walking, searching for a warm place for the night. After a mile or so she found a barn and walked up to the house, where she asked the farmer for help. He had horse blankets and a barn for Monday. For the second time, Monday cheated death.

The farmer's name was Baxter; in honor of his hospitality, Monday's owner decided to name him Baxter.

When Baxter arrived safely in Florida, Andrew instantly liked him and arranged for a client of his to purchase him. Andrew would train the horse for free, in exchange for fifty percent interest in him.

At their first show, when he and Andrew entered the schooling area, Baxter returned to the only job he truly knew. He attempted to race every horse in the area, flat out running away. Andrew never went in the show ring; it would be pointless with Baxter acting so crazy.

At the second show, the same thing happened. Baxter ran away with Andrew in the schooling ring. By the third show, the owner was sick and tired of paying the bills on a horse who was not showing. Andrew was told to enter the ring or he would lose the ride on Baxter. He complied.

Andrew was in for the shock of his life. Instead of running away with Andrew, Baxter was instantly perfect and seemed to know exactly what to do. He acted as if he had been showing his whole life. Andrew was shocked: he has never before or since had a similar experience with another horse.

Baxter won that class, and thereafter won every class in the pre-green division. His bravery and classic jumping style were indisputable. ("He is," says Andrew, "the bravest horse I've ever ridden in my life.") Baxter finished the season as circuit champion in the pre-green hunters in Ocala.

Then, as often happens in the horse industry, Andrew and the client parted company. Unfortunately, Andrew had no written contract with his client, so he had no proof that the horse was half his. Baxter left his barn, leaving Andrew heartbroken. Andrew had lost "the most incredible horse I've ever worked with."

The new trainer moved the horse into the jumper divisions. Baxter looked like a lunatic, and in addition sported a bloody mouth from the cruel bit he wore. Once again the horse had hit a bad spot, and things only got worse when his owner went broke and quit paying Baxter's board.

The owner of the farm where Baxter lived knew nothing about horses. When he did not receive his board fees, he went to his lawyer for advice. The lawyer obviously didn't know anything about horses either. He recommended that Baxter not be turned out in the field, or ridden. Since "possession is nine tenths of the law," if the owner were to steal Baxter out of the field, the farm owner would never retrieve his board fees.

The end result was that Baxter ended up no longer in a horse barn, but in a chicken coop where the roof was so low he couldn't even lift his head. Baxter lived like that for eight months.

Once again, the horse teetered on the edge of existence. His weight and condition had dropped until he was nothing but a skeleton coated in filthy skin pockmarked with oozing sores. When Baxter was auctioned off on the court house steps, his life was spared yet again. Andrew was there to save him.

Andrew spent time rehabilitating him, and getting him back into work, horrified at the fact that the horse had suffered such a hellish existence. Later that year the owner who locked Baxter in the chicken coop died in a terrible tractor incident. At least there was some justice for the horse.

The first time Andrew had Baxter, the horse would do lead changes in either direction with no problem. During their second period together, Andrew discovered that Baxter no longer did right-to-left changes. Andrew feels that it was the horse's way of punishing him for not saving him sooner from the chicken coop (although it wasn't until after Andrew bought him back that he learned Baxter had been incarcerated that way.)

Andrew was a struggling young trainer, and he cut costs wherever he could. One of his cost saving methods was to use a very cheap farrier. Unfortunately, Andrew got what he was paying for. He began showing Baxter in the pre-green division again once the horse recuperated. Baxter jumped his heart out at shows. But he had crooked front legs and was jumping on poorly shod feet. After shows, he would go "off."

One Monday, top horseman Danny Robertshaw came to try the horse. He said, "Andrew, this horse is lame."

Andrew said, "Well he's always lame on Monday morning."

And yes folks, that is how Monday got his name.

Monday was vetted several times, but never passed.

One day Andrew was simply trotting Monday around a schooling ring at West Palm Beach when the horse was spotted by Lisa Towell. The Towells: Jack, Lisa, Liza, and Hardin, own and run Finally Farm in Camden, South Carolina, and are known for producing top horses.

Lisa, the member of the Towell family known for having the best eye for a horse, knew instantly that she had to have Monday. She felt an overwhelming pull towards him; a feeling that the horse was trying to tell her that he was supposed to be with the Towells.

Lisa knew that Monday could be a star small junior hunter

44

for their daughter Liza. Liza had shown the large pony Tickled Pink to championships at both the National Pony Finals and the National Horse Show. She needed a brilliant horse to follow in those illustrious hoofprints. Lisa knew that Monday could fill those shoes.

She bugged Jack continually. "You have to call Andrew. We have to have that horse!"

Finally, several months later while they were at Devon, Jack ran into Andrew.

"Send me that horse so I can try him," Jack told Andrew. He was less interested in the horse than in getting Lisa off his back.

The first week after he came to the Towells, Monday colicked. The second week, with Geoff Teall judging, right off the bat Monday came through with scores of 88 and 90 (out of a possible 100).

Along with the high scores and incredible talent came Monday's eccentricities. He didn't want to be schooled, and he didn't allow for many practice jumps. Luckily, Dave Morris, who worked for the Towells, figured Monday out quite quickly. The horse knew his job, knew he could blow the competition away, and didn't feel the need for any practice.

Monday couldn't be worked down if he was up, instead he would get hotter. A session on the lunge, however, would solve the problem.

Watching Monday, a casual observer might think he was crazy. At Harrisburg one fall, Jack took Monday into the indoor for a school. Monday was a nut, spooking and whirling so much that Jack didn't even make it around the course. Jack left the ring disheartened and handed Monday to Dave.

"Don't worry about it," Dave told Jack. "Today's not a show day so he knows he doesn't need to be in there. He'll be fine tomorrow."

Dave nailed it. The next day, the show began. Monday strode into the ring like he owned it. He did. As Jack says, "He had springs in his back legs; there was nothing he couldn't jump."

One of Liza's biggest classes with Monday was the inaugural American Hunter-Jumper Foundation Hunter Classic, held at West Palm Beach at night under the lights. The Towells were unsure of how Monday would handle the environment.

At first, it looked a little iffy to Jack. Monday appeared to be uncomfortable with the light and shadows, shaking his head a bit. Then he disappeared into a dark spot. When he reappeared, it was evident that he had decided the lighting was no big deal. The trip was brilliant, and as Liza turned the corner to the last fence of the course, the hedges, she kicked Monday into a big gallop down the long approach. Monday jumped boldly over the hedges to a cheering crowd, top call, and a score of 95!

The class paid for Liza's first year of college.

Liza says that she could run down a long approach to a single oxer and Monday would always get there; he "made me feel like such a hero." She's tried it since on other horses—it just doesn't happen.

One year at Devon, Liza blew away all the other competitors in the Small Junior Hunter Stake. In fact, in a surprising move the judges, Susie Schoellkopf and Susie Humes, decided not to have the scores announced. It turned out that Monday had earned a 95 and the closest competitor was in the mid-eighties: the judges didn't want to embarrass them.

As Jack says, "When he was in his job, no one could beat him, and he knew it and they knew it."

In keeping with his rules, Monday was rarely ridden at home. He knew that practice was unnecessary. Jack would sit on him in the ring while teaching other lessons in order to keep Monday's back strong, but that was about the extent of home schooling.

One day Liza, who never sat on Monday at home, decided she would sneak in a ride while her parents were gone. While the stablehands looked on in astonishment, Liza led her horse out to the ring. She was back in two minutes.

Andrew had warned the Towells not to even attempt a right-to-left flying change on Monday; luckily they heeded his advice. (Liza says that as a kid at the time, she didn't think to contradict Andrew, which proved very fortunate. Now as a trainer, she thinks she would have felt compelled to fix it, and as a result, messed the horse up!)

The Towells taught Monday to always land on his left lead, as he would do left-to-right changes. As long as he landed left, he was good to go. In all the years Liza showed him, he only lost two classes due to his lack of that lead change.

The Towells are quick to point out that all the success they had with Monday couldn't have happened without their vet, Dr. Witwren and their farrier, Jimmy Misenhiener. Monday's colicky incidents continued until it was discovered that he had some kind of stone in his intestines. As Jack said, "It just showed how much heart he has, that he kept on going."

Jimmy discovered that his lameness problems were due to a separation in the wall of his hoof. Jimmy switched him to titanium shoes, which were perfect for Monday. They were strong enough to keep his feet together better than aluminum, and yet lightweight enough to show off his beautiful gaits.

After this discovery, Jimmy stuck with Monday, always showing up with his tools wherever Monday might need him, in case some dirt or a stone got caught in the separation in his hoof wall. One year at Madison Square Garden, Jack looked up to see Jimmy standing on the sidelines, tools in hand. No one had asked him to come. Jimmy showed up of his own accord, paying for the flight himself, just to be there. That was the kind of allegiance Monday inspired.

Unfortunately, the day arrived when Liza aged out of the juniors. Liza and Monday had been an unstoppable team and now that team needed to be split up. Lisa "hated it when Liza outgrew the juniors." Monday had to be sold. Everyone was heartbroken. Jack says, "Monday is by far the best horse we've ever had."

As they were in the process of selling him, Monday got sick. He no longer seemed himself. He couldn't jump in his usual athletic manner or show the brilliance that was naturally his.

A vet solved the mystery. Although at that time EPM was little heard of (and in fact many didn't even believe in its existence), Monday was diagnosed with the disease which can cripple and even kill horses. Monday faced yet again what could have been a death sentence.

Once more, he was lucky. He responded well to treatment and returned to his flawless and powerful jumping style.

While Monday and Liza were creating magic in the junior hunters, Sarah Friedman was showing a junior hunter named Magic Kingdom and competing in Medal/Maclay classes. Magic Kingdom had helped Sarah become accurate and confident in the junior hunters; now she needed a horse that could take her to the top.

She and her parents chose Monday Morning.

Sarah realized she had a lot to live up to. The previous year, Monday and Liza had been champion at Devon, Harrisburg, the Capital Challenge, Washington (D.C.) and New York. Sarah had heard that at one show, Monday had scored a 100. To top it all off, he was named Horse of the Year, beating horses from all disciplines and all breeds to become the number one horse in the country!

So it was no wonder that Sarah felt some pressure.

Monday hadn't been snapped up because, despite this illustrious career, he hadn't been looking completely sound. In addition, everyone knew Liza was a very talented rider. Most people were too scared to attempt to follow in her footsteps. So there weren't many buyers looking at Monday.

Sarah herself wasn't sure. Was the horse sound? And if he was, could she live up to what Liza had accomplished? However, the price was right at the time, so she went ahead and tried him. It was the end of the day, and nearly dark. Things went well. She and Monday clicked. Her parents proceeded with the purchase.

Right after they bought him, Monday colicked. Sarah gave him some time off.

When she began riding him again, Monday ran away with her on numerous occasions. Sarah says she's "not quite sure" why Monday did not have a stellar career at the track, because "he's very, very fast!"

Finally, they got to show, at Tampa, Florida. Although she was nervous, Sarah and Monday ended up champion. This was okay, Sarah thought. Monday was tricky and wanted things done his way, but in the show ring he gave 110 %. Although he only measured 15.2, in the ring he grew a hand higher. He had a huge stride and an unbelievable jump. He jumped so powerfully that Sarah quickly learned she had to be super tight and accurate.

She also discovered Monday's disdain for schooling. Sarah was allowed a few jumps in the warm-up ring and that was it. If she tried to do more, Monday would get hotter and hotter. He had a terrific canter and was great to ride by himself, but if there were others in the schooling area he still reverted to his racing days. In hack classes, though, he realized that he was on stage and loved the opportunity to show off.

As long as Sarah did things Monday's way, things went smoothly. She learned not to be "fussy and academic" with him. Lead changes were done Monday's way, not the way Sarah had learned. He also chose how they would approach the jumps. If Sarah didn't let him gallop while keeping a very light feel of his mouth, allowing him the freedom he wanted for his explosive, breathtaking jump, Monday could jump quite plainly. It was as if he was telling Sarah, "If you aren't going to do it my way then you can just have a mediocre jump."

At Devon, Sarah was terribly embarrassed when she "chipped her way around the course." The Towells were there, adding to the pressure in her mind.

Sarah is greatly indebted to Monday for all he taught her. Although he was picky and tough, he was also brilliant and honest. Sarah didn't need a perfect distance to get a good jump. She could get in to a fence a little bit tight or slightly bold and Monday would jump in good form and put in a good effort no matter what.

As Sarah learned how to ride Monday, the embarrassing episodes receded and they were replaced by significant success: at Lake Placid and at Vermont they were Champion, and they took Reserve at the Hampton Classic. Together they amassed a great many wins, and wins at prestigious places, including top ribbons at indoors.

Harrisburg started out well, with top ribbons in the first over fences classes. A top four placing in the stakes class would have garnered them a champion or reserve. But Sarah reverted to her old ways and picked at Monday instead of allowing him to go forward to a fence in the stakes. Monday stopped, dumping Sarah. It was a reminder to Sarah that success with Monday was dependent on following Monday's rules.

Sarah admires Monday tremendously, and, like Andrew and the Towells, is honored to have had him in her life. He was, she says, "wise beyond his years." Monday seemed to realize that, with his crooked legs (and problem feet) he could do only so much. So he gave it all in the show ring, and limited his warm-ups and lessoning.

Sarah says "he had spent years of his life with humans treating him like he was worthless, yet he never lost his faith in people. Most horses would have given up a long, long time ago, yet he never did. He was stoic enough to make it through his bad times, and ended up in good hands with people who realized how special he was, with so much heart and ability." Although his respect and fondness needed to be (understandably) earned, once it was, the recipient was forever in his good graces.

Monday became such a sweetheart that a toddler entering his stall would be in no danger. On the ground, he displayed perfect manners and eagerly waited for his butterscotch treats and ginger snaps (peppermints were not acceptable). Monday's groom, Cindy, used to keep boxes of ginger snaps all over the barn, and had some with her at all times. Cindy was well known for being a tough character who never spoiled any of her charges, yet she would sneak Monday cookies at every opportunity.

Despite his sweet disposition, Monday continued to insist that he was and always would be only a show horse. Sarah's one attempt at a trail ride was short and not something she would ever repeat.

After aging out of the junior ranks, Sarah hoped to take Monday to college and show him in the amateur-owner division. Now that they were clicking, and she had earned Monday's respect, she wanted the chance to show everyone how great they could be together. Unfortunately, Monday had begun to show his age, and had become stiff and creaky.

Sarah asked a vet to inject Monday's hocks and ankles to help him out. It proved impossible. His hocks had basically fused, and the vet couldn't get in to inject his ankles either, as they were so tight and arthritic. Sarah made the sad decision to retire Monday. Although she was terribly disappointed, she knew it wasn't fair to ask him to compete if he wasn't one hundred percent up to it physically.

With his show ring days behind him, Monday is happily retired in Connecticut. He's got a big, comfortable stall, and plenty of turn-out.

No one who saw him compete will ever forget his brilliant style, athleticism, and bravery. And no one who was associated with him will ever forget his generosity and huge heart.

51

Monday cheated death repeatedly, rising from humble be-ginnings to become one of the top hunters of all time. As Andrew says, "He was the most amazing horse I ever knew and had the most incredible lucky star."

⟿ Honoring Barbaro

In the winter of 2005-2006 a brilliant bay colt made people sit up and take notice. His speed and dominance on the track and his exciting win in the Kentucky Derby brought him worldwide fame. His tragic breakdown in the Preakness and subsequent struggle to survive soon brought him universal attention, not just from racing fans, but from everyday people in every part of the world.

Many thought the cocky bay colt would be the horse to finally capture the elusive Triple Crown. Instead, he became famous for his will to live, for his unfailingly cheerful attitude in the face of tremendous odds.

One of the people caught up in Barbaro's amazing story was Anne Phinney, a sixth-grade school teacher at the Town of Webb School in Old Forge, New York. Anne had learned that Michael Matz, whom she'd been fortunate enough to work for in the past, was training a colt that had qualified for the Kentucky Derby.

Anne had been following Michael's career, and her students had learned about Michael's incredible success in the show jumping world, and his retirement to train Thoroughbred racehorses. They began following Barbaro's career, and celebrated his win in the Florida Derby. Then the colt became the favorite to win the Derby.

He also became a teacher for the class, as Anne used the "buzz" about Barbaro during the week before the Derby to discuss horse racing with her class and teach them about the laws of probability (built around racing odds).

Barbaro's decisive win in the Derby (by the largest margin in 60 years) further piqued the students' interest. The Monday morning after his win the kids could talk of nothing else. They began keeping tabs on the horse daily. They learned about his life, about the people involved in racing, and the strategies used to keep racehorses both fit and relaxed at the same time. Soon, it felt like Barbaro was a member of the class.

The Monday morning after the Preakness, the kids once again could talk of nothing but Barbaro. Unfortunately, this time the mood had changed from exhilaration to despair. To the kids in the class, as for everyone watching, the Preakness was heartbreaking. "What went wrong?" they wanted to know. How could this horse, with whom they felt such a connection, have suffered this horrendous injury?

Anne had no answers, other than the medical facts. But as the students discussed their feelings in class, an idea began to form. There was something they could do, a way they could use the connection they felt with Barbaro to ease their anguish. In the wake of other tragedies, such as the attack on the World Trade Center on September 11th, Anne had had her students draw pictures as a form of therapy.

They would do the same thing now. The class would put together a student-illustrated picture book of Barbaro's first three years of life. They brainstormed and chose events of the horse's life leading up to the Kentucky Derby and then on to the Preakness. Students then picked which event he or she wished to illustrate. By the end of that day, most of the students were deeply engrossed in the project. Everyone's spirits lifted as Barbaro's life began to emerge from the pages.

As it took shape, the class decided that they would send the book to Michael Matz along with a get-well card for Barbaro. They knew that Barbaro was receiving thousands of cards, treats, and e-mails from around the world and were not expecting a response. Their goal was to offer comfort to the horse and his family, and to give themselves a sense of contribution, of creating something good out of something so horrifying.

Among the events or scenes the students chose to draw were: the outside front entrance of New Bolton festooned with get-well cards and flowers sent by well-wishers, Barbaro in the raft as he was coming out of surgery, and Barbaro looking over a field of babies—his future babies.

Two weeks later, Anne received a memo in her mailbox. Gretchen Jackson, (Barbaro's owner, along with her husband Roy) had called. Anne was astonished! She couldn't believe she had gotten a call from Gretchen.

Returning the call, she learned that Michael had made a copy of the book and given it to the Jacksons. Gretchen was so appreciative. She wanted Anne to assure the children that she and Roy were in it for the long haul, that as long as Barbaro was not in pain, they would do whatever it took to save their horse.

Gretchen told Anne that Barbaro seemed to understand that the humans were trying to help him. He was a perfect patient. Gretchen also said that she and her family were overwhelmed and touched by the outpouring of love and support for Barbaro.

The response from Gretchen thrilled the class. Knowing that they were able to provide her some comfort during this devastating experience both empowered and uplifted them.

During the summer, Anne went to a benefit for the Barbaro Fund in Saratoga. The fund raised money for the New Bolton Center, where Barbaro was being treated. There she was reunited with Michael Matz, a very special occasion for her! She had worked for him while he was competing the incomparable Jet Run, and it was great to get caught up with Michael. Not only is he an incredible trainer, but an incredible human being as well. (Michael is well known for his heroism after the crash of United Flight 232 in 1989, when he rescued four children from the burning wreckage.)

At the benefit Anne met Dean Richardson, Barbaro's vet. She was extremely impressed by this "down-to-earth, caring person." Richardson told her, "If this horse could be well on well wishes, he would be well now." The connection that the class felt with Barbaro was a connection that was echoed around the world.

Anne also met the Jacksons, who thanked her once more for the Barbaro book her class had created.

The book brought the class more attention when they were featured in an HBO special about Barbaro. The experience, Anne says, was "over the top." Old Forge, New York, is a small, isolated town. To be included in a television special was a "wonderful experience for these kids as a result of a wonderful horse."

Anne's "Barbaro" class is now in high school, and although they were, like all of us, devastated when Barbaro lost his fight for life, they have been kept up-to-date on all the changes he has been responsible for. The legacy the colt has left behind has been termed "The Barbaro Effect." Racetrack surfaces are being changed to softer material that is kinder to fragile bones and tendons. Research into laminitis has been well funded and continues to expand. The Barbaro Fund, started by an anonymous donor, has raised well over $1 million to benefit New Bolton Center. The backstretch workers—the grooms and stall cleaners that work on the track—have also benefited with better living and working conditions.

The FOBs (Fans of Barbaro) have saved more than 2100 horses and raised more than $850,000 in support of a better life for horses. Founder and exercise rider Alex Brown describes the FOBs as "a community dedicated to honoring his legacy by improving the welfare of horses and the humans involved with them." Alex says "Barbaro has really given all of us a good kick in the withers. Horse racing can't just do things the same old way. People care now. People are looking." To learn more, check out the website (www.alexbrownracing.com).

Barbaro never got the opportunity to win the Triple

Crown. Instead, he did something greater; he improved the lives of current and future racehorses as well as those who care for them. As student Allie McCumber says, "Barbaro might be gone, but his legend will live forever."

⤳ Easy Otie Whiz

Into all our lives comes one special horse who is our "horse of a lifetime." For Matt Mills, that horse is Easy Otie Whiz.

For starters, Easy is stunning. His dark bay coat shimmers; his refined head and soft eye speak of his intelligence and kindness.

"It's almost like he can read my mind," Matt Mills says about the stallion that took him to team gold in reining at the 2006 World Equestrian Games in Aachen, Germany.

Matt trains for Out West Stallion Station and Performance Horses in Scottsdale, Arizona, owned by Bobbie and David Cook. To say that he loves his job would be a serious understatement. Matt declares, "I'm having so much fun doing this I can't even describe it. I get up in the morning and I can't wait to get here."

Although Matt competed as a youth rider in such events as western pleasure and trail, reining became his passion. After experiencing his first slide, he says, "I was speechless; I was grinning from ear to ear."

Matt and his wife Karen had followed Easy's career, never failing to be impressed by the magnificent bay colt. Easy's extraordinary looks and tremendous talent had attracted several interested buyers, but his owner, Frank, refused to sell. No matter what they offered, the answer always was the same. "No, he's not for sale."

Easy had been shown by pro Duane Latimer for his three- and four-year-old seasons, doing extremely well with him. Frank then began to show him. Easy did equally well, proving to Matt just how special the stallion is. Few horses can move from a pro to a non-pro that seamlessly, particularly since Frank was still rather a novice rider. Easy appeared to grasp the situation, and although still a youngster himself, he took care of Frank by showing him the ropes and doing a phenomenal job despite Frank's inexperience.

In 2005, Bobbie Cook needed a replacement for one of her breeding stallions. Karen suggested they consider Easy. Matt spotted Frank at a show a short time later and approached him about Easy. Matt admits, "We must have timed it just right." Not only was Easy available, but he was within the price range the farm had set for a new stallion. In no time Easy had moved into his new quarters at Out West.

Generally, Matt feels it takes him a little time to gel with a horse, for the horse and Matt to get to know each other. With Easy it was as if they had known each other all along. From the first day Matt sat on him he had complete confidence in the stallion. He felt as though he could show him anywhere and be immediately competitive.

The connection they established was obviously apparent to the judges as well, for 2005 was a year of tremendous success for Matt and Easy. In their first show together, they were second in the Open Division, scoring a 147 ½. They were just getting started. They took the Intermediate Open Classic Championship at the National Reining Breeders Classic in Katy, Texas (winning $60,000 in the process!), were third in Senior Reining at the AQHA World show, third in the NRHA Derby Intermediate Open division, and took both Intermediate Open Champion and Open Reserve Champion at Reining by the Bay in Woodside, California.

Matt says Easy is "just rock solid. I never did practice runs with him; he always came out ready to show. His whole career he was just right there." Easy was so confident in his abilities that after finishing a run he would walk out of the arena and yawn as big as he possibly could, as if to say, "Is that it? Was that all I had to do?"

Judges, other competitors, and spectators alike could not fail to miss Easy's charisma. Fans were attracted to his athleticism, his presence, and the fact that, as Matt says, he's "darn sure pretty."

Matt put Easy's beauty and presence to good use, showcasing it in a pattern by standing Easy for several seconds at a time in the middle of the ring. With his dark bay coat glittering in the coliseum lights, the superbly muscled stallion demanded everyone's attention. Easy, Matt says, "could stand there all day, like a statue. So I took advantage of that."

After the tremendous successes of 2005, Matt's thoughts turned to the World Equestrian Games coming up in Aachen in 2006. He and Easy headed to the qualifier being held at the Kentucky Horse Park in Lexington.

The line-up included the top reining competitors in the world. Looking over the list, Matt realized what an extremely tough competition it would be. It was enough to shake anybody's confidence. Yet Matt felt fine. His confidence in Easy had become an unshakable faith. Easy was always on his job. Throughout his career he was always there for Matt, always there for his other riders. All Matt needed to do was do his job.

He did. They received the highest score of Matt's career, 231 ½. In doing so, he and Easy were the winners of the whole competition, qualifying for the World Equestrian Games and garnering the title of USEF Reining Champion.

Easy now was seven, an age when some reining horses start to lose their edge, to no longer have the fire and speed to make it at the top of the discipline. Not Easy. He came out stronger than ever.

Which was good, because they were going to Germany!

The experience of competing at the World Equestrian

Games was unlike anything Matt had felt as a reiner. Generally, reining is a very individual sport, and riders are intensely competitive with one another. At the WEG, as part of a team, the dynamics were entirely different. Matt loved it. The opening and closing ceremonies alone were an incredible experience. Forty thousand spectators watched and cheered. None of the riders had ever had the chance to be on stage like that!

The events themselves were "electric," with 10,000 wild fans screaming in the bleachers. And fans included competitors from other disciplines, who all seized the opportunity to watch the top riders in the world compete in disciplines other than their own.

Easy and Matt, and the other members of the American team, took home the Reining Gold Medal. For Matt it was "the most exhilarating feeling I've ever had with a horse. You have the best of every Olympic discipline there, and it was so much fun to be part of a team."

In the individual runs, Matt and Easy scored a 224 ½, just missing out on the bronze medal. Easy's magnetic personality charmed everyone, creating a mob scene of both press and spectators alike after his performance, all eager for a chance to meet this star. And it wasn't just in Germany: throughout Easy's life, a host of people have followed his career.

After Germany, Matt and Easy headed to Spain for the Mallorca Western Festival. Easy was shipped by barge across the Mediterranean Sea to the island. As soon as the horse stepped off the barge, Matt knew Easy wasn't right. The sparkle was gone from his eye and he looked exhausted. For three days, Easy fought a fever. Although Easy improved and the vet managed to get the fever down, the stallion was not himself for the competition. He still scored a respectable 217 ½, but he never fired. Matt says "It was the only show in Easy's life where he didn't turn it on, and it was only because he'd been sick."

Easy came back home to Arizona to be retired from competition and become a stud. There was nothing left for him to prove, nothing "big enough for me to show him in," declares Matt.

It's not just Easy's talent and beauty that make Matt so proud of him. Easy is a stallion that never acts like one. The horse is so gentle that Matt trusts him with his two-year-old son. Easy's kind eye and gentle demeanor make everyone who sees him want to walk up and pet him.

Always eager for affection, in the barn Easy nickers to Matt. "Come and spend time with me, pet me, feed me peppermints." Easy is not just a competitive partner and top stud: he is Matt's pet.

That doesn't mean Matt no longer rides him. Matt loves riding Easy because "he's so much fun. I've never had another horse like him. I'm all about winning but riding him is so much fun that the fun is what matters."

If Matt is having a rough day, or a tough time with another horse, his remedy is to go hop on Easy. Sometimes he'll ride the horse with a bridle, sometimes he'll go bridleless. But one thing remains constant. After riding Easy, life is always better.

Matt is very generous about letting other people ride Easy. He has so much faith in the horse that he doesn't hesitate to offer.

People are surprised that Matt is willing to let them ride this world-class horse, and then further surprised that initially Easy appears lazy. "This is that high-powered, super speedy horse?" they wonder. Instead, Easy acts like a dude ranch mount.

Then Matt unveils the secret. "You have to put your foot on the gas." As soon as the riders do, the Ford Focus they were sitting on morphs into a Formula One racecar. Now they recognize the Easy who won a reining Gold Medal.

Easy has been retired to stud for three years now. Many of his foals sport his big, soft eye, his kindness, and his talent. Matt is just starting Easy's first crop. "Not all of them are going to be great," says Matt, "but a lot of them are going to be very nice."

Before Easy, Matt had never experienced the feeling that he gets when he rides him. He has not felt it since on any other horse. He declares, "I'm still trying to find another horse like him."

OVERSEAS

TRAINING WITH ULLA SALZGEBER

How many of us dream of going to Europe and training with a top coach, maybe even an Olympic calibre one? Most of us just talk about it. Then there are those that make that dream a reality.

With three of her horses, Virginia Leary took off for Germany for two months one winter, to train with Ulla Salzgeber. Those two months changed her life.

Initially, Virginia was a bit worried. Was she good enough? Now in her 50's, she wondered if she would be up to the physical demands. Were her horses good enough? The thought of riding with Ulla Salzgeber was intimidating to say the least.

Virginia had been riding and training event horses, and teaching event riders, for 35 years. She had gotten over wanting to "throw myself off of a cliff with horses." Although she'd loved it, now she wanted to do something different, to immerse herself in learning dressage. Virginia is passionate about learning and growing, and in Ulla she knew she had found someone who shared her passion. Virginia wanted to get herself into the ranks of the FEI (Federation Equestre Internationale) riders, and this was her chance to do it.

She had chosen Ulla as the European she wanted to train with for several reasons. They had met a decade ago when Virginia accompanied Mary Alice Malone on a trip to Europe to look at stallions. She'd been impressed with how nice Ulla was.

Shortly thereafter, articles in *The Chronicle of the Horse* and other publications began to surface, relating Ulla's success. Virginia would read them and think "that was that nice woman in Germany. She's doing *really* well."

Soon Ulla became a star on the international dressage scene with her now famous Rusty. Together they won Team Gold and Individual Bronze in the 2000 Sydney Olympics and Team Gold and Individual Silver in the 2004 Atlanta Olympics, besides being European Champions twice.

So Virginia was excited when an FEI trainers/judges forum that she attended along with Ann Guptill (whom she credits with helping transition her from eventing coach to dressage coach) was taught by Ulla.

It was, she says, "Awesome! The best thing I've ever been to." That was when the idea of going to Europe to train with Ulla Salzgeber started to take hold in her mind.

When Virginia learned that Ulla would be teaching a clinic in neighboring Washington, Connecticut, she immediately called to try to get in. "No way," she was told. "The clinic is already completely booked. You'll never get in."

Virginia, undaunted, begged. She knew that the big name dressage riders would have first dibs, and she wasn't among them. But, she was going. It was right in her own backyard. There was no way she was going to miss it.

The answer was still no. "Take my name. Maybe there will be a cancellation," Virginia told the woman. But the secretary didn't see much hope in that.

Two weeks later, Virginia got a call. "You're in."

Then, Virginia started to doubt herself. "Am I good enough?" she wondered. "This woman is an Olympic Gold Medalist! Can I really ride with her?"

The clinic only whetted her appetite for training with Ulla. It was a decisive moment, because Virginia realized that this was what she was looking for. She had to take the plunge. But would Ulla agree to take her on?

She asked Ulla if she could come. The answer was yes! Ulla didn't care whether or not Virginia was the best rider. What mattered was whether Virginia wanted to improve and if she was willing to work hard to make it happen. About that, there was no question.

So, plans were made. Virginia and her horses would head to Europe in January. It was so far away, it didn't seem real to Virginia. And the idea was very scary. During the ensuing months she had plenty of time to chicken out. But she stuck to her plan.

She was met at JFK Airport by her International Racehorse Transportation agent, Claudia Fredrichs. They decided to make a day of it, visiting New York City and going out to dinner. It was a bad idea. There was a big traffic accident and they couldn't find their way back to JFK. They were lost on Long Island while the clock was ticking towards take-off; they barely made it back in time to load the horses.

Normally not a good flyer, Virginia found that this trip was different. It was so quiet, and her horses were in very capable hands, so she found herself able to sleep on the flight over. It seemed unreal to her that she was truly on her way.

When she arrived in Germany, she was able to get settled in to the hotel by midnight. That was when it started to get really lonely. There was no one else in the hotel. Virginia unpacked and then went online: e-mail, it turned out, kept her alive throughout her adventure. It was not easy to call home too often with the time differences. But the little messages she got first thing in the morning when everyone at home was asleep kept her feeling connected.

The next morning Ulla herself picked up Virginia and took her to get a rental car. Virginia could barely believe it. She got in her rental car and headed back to Bad Worishofen by Navisystem. She called friends to let them know she was really driving down the Autobahn by herself! It was a beautiful, sunny day, and a great introduction to Germany.

Three horses came with Virginia to Germany: Lexus, a big Dutch Prix St. Georges horse; Kells, her Irish Spotted horse (who made quite an impression); and a young horse, Oliver.

She had chosen to go during the winter because it was a slow time both for her and for Ulla. Virginia was "Ulla's winter project."

Ulla had a schedule all set for her new student. The first month they would focus on Prix St. Georges; the second month on Intermediaire. First, there were changes to be made in Virginia's position. Ulla says, "If your position is right, and your aids are right, it all works."

The changes were hard; they made Virginia feel "like a beginner again, very awkward." Yet just as Ulla said, as soon as Virginia sat well and used her aids right, her horse went correctly.

The changes not only were hard, but they made Virginia quite sore initially. She wasn't used to using her chest and abdomen so much. Luckily the town, Bad Worishofen, is built on hot springs and Ulla's husband owns a spa/hotel, so relaxing baths and therapeutic massages were available to rejuvenate Virginia's tired body.

Ulla expected Virginia to do it right, so Virginia learned how to do it right. She found Ulla's teaching "a very clear system, easy to understand."

According to Ulla, "when the system is clear, the horses go correctly." The training is "very dynamic and fluid, very forward, and the horses get really fit and strong." The horses must be "responsive off the aids at all times." In fact, so responsive that Ulla says, "you can fix anything in one stride."

By giving Virginia eight things to correct at once, by requiring more, Virginia learned to give more. As she learned this, doing the eight things at once became easy, and she was able to do still more.

Teaching in Germany is, reports Virginia, "much more direct. There is no coddling of clients. Ulla gave me six balls to hold up in the air at once. It's very tough, but when you get it right, she's there for you!" And because she's so exacting, when Ulla "tells you you did something well, you know it's *really* good!"

The work was so demanding that Virginia, accustomed to riding five to six horses a day, rode only her two FEI horses and was exhausted. Her two month stay there resulted in a loss of 20 pounds.

Virginia says that Ulla was "so great to take me on and so good to me." She gave Virginia lessons seven days a week. "She worked so hard for me, she gave me herself 100%."

Virginia found it astonishing to watch Ulla ride. The horses were all so quick off her aids; Ulla was "on a different level than anyone I've ever seen. She only rides for 9's and 10's. She's very intense."

And she gets what she rides for. In defending her European championship in 2003, Ulla and Rusty scored an astounding 85.44 in the Grand Prix Freestyle.

If Virginia wasn't riding, she was watching Ulla ride. In fact, she was so immersed in the atmosphere that at one point Ulla basically told her to get out of the barn. "Go see some castles!" she said.

The second month was so intense, it was like starting all over again. But Virginia ate it up. "It was such a privilege, having fun and learning, it was so exciting to be learning again. It was like going back to college!" She feels that dressage has a particular fascination for her because, "as long as the horses are sound, they can always do it better."

The changes Ulla made in her position resulted in an incredible difference in Virginia's horses. Ulla uses mirrors a lot, as well as videotapes, so that she and her students can constantly observe themselves in order to improve their positions and use of the aids.

One of Virginia's main challenges stemmed from her eventing background. She found it very difficult to keep collecting her horses. In eventing, she was always asking horses to open their strides. Now she had to learn to do just the opposite.

At one point, she attended a show in Vienna with the Salzgebers. She wasn't showing, just spectating, and found herself quite surprised at what she saw. She had assumed, as many of us would have, that all German horses lived in impeccable barns, doing impeccable dressage.

This show, the equivalent of a small CDI, had some very good horses, and some "just horses." Her fear that everything in Germany was better proved unfounded.

Germany does have backyard barns. And their horses are not all perfect dressage horses. Looking out at a field at one point, Virginia spied a string of western trail horses heading out in a hack line.

She also learned about just what stalwart campaigners the Europeans are. During her stay with Ulla, it was winter in Germany: very cold, very icy. Yet shows continued: no one bailed because of the weather.

At Ulla's barn, there are no tricks, no gadgets. In fact, Ulla rides in a snaffle most of the time. Intense as she is, she has a good time. Ulla says, "Good marks come from a horse having fun."

Virginia hadn't been too sure about taking her Irish Sport horse with her: a cross between a Thoroughbred stallion (Conquistador Cielo) out of a colored draft mare. She wondered how he would be received, and how he would do. Would a big, loud pinto fit in among all the fancy warmbloods?

Not everyone thought so. Ulla's vet saw the horse and said "I see you are training circus horses now."

Salzgeber was nonplussed. "All horses," she stresses, "can be made better through dressage."

The Irish horse proved her point. He just got "better and better, lighter and more elastic." He "came to work every day." Kells is hot, so Ulla worked with Virginia, teaching her how to bring out the best in a hot horse.

Always, Ulla encouraged her to strive for more, to say to each horse, "You can give me more."

And although Ulla is obviously a fabulous rider and competitor, Virginia says she "has the fire in her teaching! She loves to teach!"

When Virginia returned to Connecticut, she found that the lessons she had learned worked just as well on students' Thoroughbred event horses as they did on the warmblood dressage horses. Scores have been lowered (event horses are scored on penalties so lower scores are better scores), horses have become more supple and responsive. Virginia says the results "have been nothing less than dramatic."

Virginia's teaching, too, has improved, clarified thanks to Ulla's tutelage.

Summing it up, Virginia says, "It was the hardest thing I've ever done, and the best thing I've ever done."

~⅔ In the Land of Genghis Khan

Genghis Khan, along with his successors, established the largest contiguous empire in history, spanning the entire Asian continent from the Pacific Ocean to modern day Hungary in Europe. How did Mongolia reach this point of power, of domination of so much of the world?

The engine of this world power was the Mongolian horse.

Mongolian horses are small, tough, and wild. They are not kept in barns or tethered on lines. They remain, like their owners, unshackled, free to roam at will. They retain a fiery, independent spirit that serves both them, and their riders, well.

When Genghis Khan decided to expand his empire, the horses were the key to his success. At that time European warfare was conducted in a ponderous fashion. Heavy horses and their riders wore suits of iron which loaded them down and made speed close to impossible. There were rules and codes of conduct to follow.

Genghis blithely dispensed with those rules and came up with his own, brilliant strategy. On his little, unencumbered horses, he could strike like lightning, run circles around other armies, and be gone before his opponents knew what had happened. Genghis' cavalry was the swiftest and most resilient ever known, and his fighting style was so phenomenal that General Douglas MacArthur studied his tactics.

There is no doubt that Genghis Khan and his successors

were mercenary. Yet that is not all there is to the story. Khan took a statesmen's approach to life. Defeated peoples were given the right to surrender. In exchange for their lives, they were required to enter into a trade agreement with Khan. Followers were highly rewarded. If a person was doing a good job at his post at the time of the conquest, that person was allowed to remain on task. Khan sought out talented, hard working people. He pioneered the concept of religious tolerance, and he put women in powerful positions. He married at nine and stayed loyal to his wife for life.

Khan was the most powerful conqueror the world has ever seen, and it was all due to the horse.

Yet the Mongolian horses have played a far bigger role than just that of warrior. They are part of the infrastructure of Mongolian culture. As nomads, the Mongolians use their horses for travel. They drink the mare's milk (ayrag), a staple of their society. The horses are used for pleasure as well, for games and for races.

For all these reasons, horses are revered. They are appreciated for the blessings they bring to the community. In Mongolia, by rights, everyone should know how to ride a horse.

Bridget Colman had been thinking about Mongolia: it seemed a fascinating and remote area of the planet to explore. The Colman family plans a big trip to out-of-the-way places every year. Bridget and her daughter Allegra love to take trips on horseback. Horses, says Bridget, "give people a real entrée to so many communities, and give you such freedom."

When she sat down with her daughter Allegra to discuss where to go, Bridget's idea became reality. With no prompting, Allegra said "I want to ride in Mongolia."

So the family set off: Bridget and her husband Mark, along with daughters Allegra and Mia.

Before leaving, the family did a lot of homework, studying the history, geography, and customs of the place.

Bridget chose the Trans Siberian railroad as their entrée

into the country, envisioning a slow transition from one culture into another. They emerged in Mongolia's capital, and only major city, Ulan Bator.

Although Mark and Mia were not big riders, Bridget and Allegra were. They took to the freedom of the country with glee. Much of the riding they'd done in the United States was bounded by insurance regulations and organizational rules. None of that existed in Mongolia.

Allegra wanted to just jump on a pony and gallop away, and she wasted no time in doing just that. At one point she galloped by a Mongolian rider, her long, blonde hair streaming in the wind. Bridget smiled as the rider looked on in astonishment at this unusual sight! Allegra seized every opportunity to race across the country, and Bridget relished the chance to do the same.

Although the Colmans felt huge on the small horses, they found them to be surefooted beyond belief. Their short, upright gaits were not comfortable, but they could gallop through and clamber over rocks without a second's hesitation. They were, says Bridget, "just like ponies, 'yeah I rule, but you can get on top.'"

The saddles proved less than inviting. They might be Russian or Mongolian, leather or wood, but they were uniformly uncomfortable. Two girths were used, like a western saddle. Sometimes after riding, the Colmans hurt so much from the saddles that they would be sore for hours. In addition to the hardness of the tack the saddles created a different angle to the hips when riding than the family was used to. This contributed to their discomfort as well.

The Mongolians wear long coats when riding; Bridget theorized that perhaps that provides padding for them while they're in the saddle!

Despite the vast open spaces, Mongolians ride single file, one behind another.

Many elements of horse handling and care have been unchanged for hundreds of years, including the way they are caught:

with loops on the end of 12-foot-long bamboo poles.

The family hired a guide, who served as their translator as well. At one point, the horse Allegra was on started bucking like a rodeo bronc. All Bridget could think was "Here's my daughter with no helmet on, riding a horse that is bucking like a maniac, and we're on rocks—oh my God!"

The guide said nothing, but he didn't take his eyes off Allegra. Eventually, Allegra could no longer stick with the horse, and came off. Undeterred, she bounced right back up and got on another horse.

The guide turned to Bridget and nodded towards Allegra. "She's welcome here any time," he said.

The Colmans were thrilled by the sight of thousands of horses of all colors milling around the encampments. Despite the fact that the horses are free, they don't roam far. They are allowed to remain unfettered and independent as a matter of respect. The rest of the livestock, including goats, sheep, and yak, roam free as well.

The Mongolian horses are not named. They are called by their color, and there are hundreds of names for colors. One can see in the horse's eyes, says Bridget, their knowledge, "Hey we're the reason Mongolia was such a power, we are pivotal to history!"

Watching them, the family got a notion of the hierarchy of a group of horses, the dynamics, and the fact that horses really like to be in groups. They were majestic, and Bridget realized what an honor it is to ride, to be allowed to sit on top of a horse. Horses let us ride them; they don't have to let themselves be ridden.

Although the Mongolians are nomadic, it is not in the sense that one might normally think. "Nomad" typically brings to mind the picture of a tribe constantly wandering, always on the move. In actuality the Mongols move back and forth between their summer and winter camps, and they always know where these camps will be.

Coming from a culture so imbued with horses, Mongolians carry over their riding style to the way they drive. Hence, to them the idea of a road is nonsense—they just drive anywhere they feel like it!

The Colmans stayed with the tribe's patriarch, in a tent located along a river in "an extraordinarily beautiful site." One morning they awakened to see a father and his five-year-old son herding their horses across the river. It was a scene they will never forget.

The horses were the ideal way to see Mongolia, as they have the best kind of four-wheel-drive. The Colmans saw unique ecosystems and wildlife including herds of reindeer, the Gobi desert, and a "glacier" the size of a bathtub. Riding across the steppes, they saw gymnastic goats performing back flips. On one ride they encountered a 70-year-old woman who was riding across the country. They also encountered the native Mongolian Prezwalski horses, which have unique DNA and are not related to western horses.

One of the major Mongolian traditions is the summer festivity called Nadaam, a giant tournament, similar to a country fair which is held on different weekends. Each one holds a horse race with over 20 riders aged five to 11, many of them bareback. One unique feature of these races is that the last rider gets a prize too, which results in some rather interesting strategies from the participants.

The Colmans found Mongolia to be a place of amazing contrast, a confluence of traditional and modern values. In some ways it was wild and untamed, and still carried on ancient traditions. Yet, cell phones were ubiquitous!

People treat horses differently everywhere, integrating them into their worlds in a myriad of ways. Seeing a country on horseback, says Bridget, is the best way to go. No matter where in the world you ride, you end up in some pretty fantastic places.

The Colmans have ridden in many countries. Yet, although the approaches are different, there is always something that remains the same: that thread which connects horse people everywhere.

Pony Tales

⤴ My Thriller

She's one of those horse angels that are a blessing to horses and people alike. A science teacher by profession, Cindy Bellis-Jones uses her 50 acre Fox Run Farm in Paris, Kentucky to rescue approximately 100 ponies a year. She's been doing it for more than 30 years now and describes her actions as "an addiction."

Cindy rescues her ponies from many different stockyards. She has rescued thousands of ponies, but My Thriller was one of the worst cases she had ever seen. A walking, coughing, skeleton with green goo oozing from his nose, My Thriller was extremely ill. Not only ill but injured as well. With a two-foot gash across his chest covered in maggots, he was a candidate, it seemed, only for the killers.

Yet he caught Cindy's eye. It was more than just her desire to rescue the pony; the more she looked at him, the more Cindy realized that this was a fabulous pony that had unfortunately landed in dire straits.

She had come to the auction that day to help find a pony to purchase for a friend's daughter. When the friend saw Cindy's attention directed at Thriller, she reacted with disdain.

"You're not thinking of *that* pony, are you?" asked the friend. She wasn't. Thriller was an unbroken two-year-old pinto, not at all appropriate for the friend's child. But he was definitely coming home with Cindy.

Thriller's name on the Coggins test, "Little Dummy,"

didn't fit at all. Cindy quickly discovered just what a clever little fellow he was.

After his arrival at Fox Run Farm, the pony spent his first month in isolation. At the time his color was a washed-out dun.

With Cindy's love and care, Thriller underwent a metamorphosis. His horrendous injury healed with barely a perceptible scar, he put on weight and developed muscle, and his dull coat changed to midnight with white splotches.

Thriller turned out to be a real people pony, a pony with a heart of gold that Cindy and her daughter Heather fell in love with. In addition, he proved to be very athletic: a good mover and an excellent jumper. Breaking him was easy; Cindy and Heather played with him and made it all into a game. Thriller was an "A student" who never did anything wrong.

After Cindy heals and trains her rescues, she sells them for basically what she put into them. Thriller was for sale for $800. Yet no one wanted him. Cindy told one potential buyer after another, "This is the best pony I've had in years." All potential buyers seemed to notice was that the pony had a long back and matching splints on his legs. Cindy found it incredibly frustrating: she had a terrific pony and somehow all people could see were his faults!

Heather had been looking for a 4-H pony to compete on, but had not chosen Thriller because she felt, that at 5'9", she was too big for the 13.3 hand pony. But after hearing all this nonsense from tire kickers, she got mad. She loved this pony. She was going to prove to these naysayers just what he was capable of!

She showed Thriller in local and 4-H shows and then took him to the Kentucky State Horse Show in July, where they won their whole division. People watching in the stands wanted to know, "Who is that pony? Who bred him?" To both Cindy and Heather, this was miraculous. A year ago, the pony had had two feet in the grave. Now he was champion at the big state horse show and everyone wanted to know where he'd come from!

Not only was Thriller competitive, he had an amazing attitude as well. Cindy said "he works so hard, he gives everything he has and does it with a smile. He's just a sweetheart, never a bad boy."

Now that Thriller had proven himself, the tables turned and those who had criticized him wanted to buy him. But that wasn't going to happen. They'd had their chance and they'd blown it. Cindy interviewed various people and in time sold him to a woman whose daughter, Mara Kranz, would show him.

Mara and My Thriller wiped up, winning top ribbons at the 2003 Pony Finals in the Large Green Pony Hunter Division, as well as the championship for Large Ponies in Zone 5 for several years in a row. Mara is a phenomenal rider and Cindy says she "did a great job with him!"

Meanwhile, back in East Windsor, New Jersey, the Rubin family was searching for a pony. Jessie Rubin had a great pony named Joey that she planned to take with her to Ocala. But Joey had gotten hurt. Although he would get better, Larry and Teri Rubin decided they wanted to purchase an additional, more advanced, pony for their daughter.

The family searched. Searched hard. They looked everywhere. On several occasions, they nearly purchased a pony, but it always fell through.

At the time they were training with Frank Hernandez of The Main Event. Frank had a close friend, Lance Williamson, who often brought horses and ponies by for Frank's clients to try out for purchase.

One day Jessie and her dad arrived at The Main Event to see Lance's van parked there. As they walked into the barn they spotted Thriller. He looked right at them and started neighing. He knew who he wanted to go home with.

Jessie and her father liked the pony's eye. Although it was late and they couldn't try him that night, they decided they would try him the next day.

The trial ride went well, very well. Jessie rode him over

bigger and bigger fences and felt comfortable and confident. He was quickly vetted, passed, and purchased. One week to go before the 2006 Ocala HITS series, and they had found their pony.

The show hosts a five week series: Jessie Rubin and her new pony, with only a week to get to know each other, showed in four of the weeks and won both the Children's Pony Hunter and Children's Equitation for the series.

Thriller then sustained both a serious head injury from a trailer incident, and an abscess. He had to be laid up for six months. Despite that, he finished 7th in Zone 2 and 1st in the Marshall & Sterling League and the Monmouth County Horse Show series for 2006.

Jessie says Thriller is the "sweetest pony. He's all business. You don't have to lunge him, you just tack him up and go out there and do it."

Larry finds him "incredibly unique, the most even tempered, kind pony I've ever seen, and he really wants to please." He's also "very professional. He goes in the ring, does his thing, comes back out and waits until his next round." Although, Larry adds, "he does expect a Mento when he comes out!"

Jessie loves Thriller, and Thriller gives that love right back to her. Once Thriller slipped on some ice that was hidden in the ring, and fell on Jessie. He got to his feet and went right to her, nuzzling her. "Are you okay? Are you hurt?" he seemed to ask.

Larry is "So thankful he's alive, that someone saved him. He's so loveable and eager to do whatever you want."

Jessie and Thriller, who train with Crystal Young of Chickadee Farm, came back in a big way in 2007. They had 22 over fences wins in a row! At the Zone 2 finals held in Harrisburg, Pennsylvania, they took the Grand Championship, with the single highest points of the show.

Things have changed at Fox Run Farm. After all those months of trying to get people interested in Thriller who instead found fault with him, and turned him down, there's a real change in tune.

When people come to Fox Run Farm now, the first thing they ask is, "Do you have a pony like Thriller?"

╌╌⊰ Dazzle

With most of the hair on his head turning grey, Dazzle could do with a bottle of "Just for Men." He's lost so many teeth that his meals consist of a "senior/Dengie mush." But there isn't a single rider at Twin Lakes Farm in Bronxville, New York that doesn't know Dazzle Me.

There are 32 school horses at Twin Lakes, yet all of the kids start on Dazzle. The 14.3 hand black Pony of the Americas mix looks, according to farm manager Scott Tarter, like "a blown up tick." But that doesn't stop him from being everybody's favorite, the one all the kids come looking for. Scott and Dazzle started teaching kids to ride at the same time: in 1984. That, says Scott, means that they both "have the same amount of experience."

Dazzle retired from jumping when he was 30, but continues to teach walk/trot and walk/trot/canter lessons. Despite his age, he does just fine with no shoes and no medication. The opinionated pony goes in a twisted wire bit, because, without it, there's no stopping him! He's so important to the school that he lives in Course Designer's old stall, the very horse that had been Greek Neff's famous show horse.

Maureen Burke, now an instructor at the barn, showed Dazzle in 1994 when she was competing in the short stirrup divisions. Others who learned to ride on him have returned to Twin Lakes with their kids, who are learning on the very same pony.

Maureen says Dazzle is so good, if he could speak English, he would be able to do her job. In fact, when Scott threatens to sell him (asking price, $4 million), she tells him that if Dazzle leaves, she "goes with him!"

Originally, two black ponies, Devil and Dazzle, taught children at Twin Lakes. Former students come home after college graduation, looking for Devil and Dazzle. Sadly, Scott tells them that Devil is no longer with them. People's faces fall in disappointment. They assume that perhaps Dazzle, too, has departed. But, Scott tells them, "take a look in the indoor."

And there goes Dazzle, running away with someone!

⤳ BARNEY

By Brent Kelley, D.V.M.
Printed originally in *The Thoroughbred Times*

"Doc, I got things to do over at the mare barn. I'll see you there when you're done here." Rufus seemed unusually downcast.

Rufus was the farm manager: a working farm manager. Nothing ever was done to a horse at Woodhill Farm unless Rufus was present. This is the way it had been for the seven or eight years I had been the farm's veterinarian, and I had been told it had been that way ever since Rufus was named manager more than 20 years before.

But here he was, telling me to do what I needed to do here at Barn 3, which houses the pleasure horses and pensioners, without overseeing the work.

Rufus drove off over the hill. I turned to Whitey, Rufus's assistant, and said, "I never thought I'd be able to touch a horse on this farm without Rufe watching me."

"He just ain't got the heart for it, Doc," Whitey replied.

"Heart for what?"

"Mrs. Wharton says to put Barney down."

I could not believe it. I asked Whitey to repeat what he had said.

"Are you sure?" I asked.

"Yeah, Doc, I'm afraid so," Whitey answered. "The old guy's just not getting around like he used to, and he's not seeing too good; he's bumping into trees and stuff."

I walked into the barn and down the aisle to Barney's stall. The old boy was peacefully chewing on hay. In all the years I had known him, everything Barney did was done peacefully.

A plain brown gelding with a small star on his forehead, Barney was about the size of a Welsh pony, but a little more refined. He was around 32 years old, and we were fairly sure that Mrs. Wharton, Woodhill's owner, was the only person who could remember a day when Barney was not on the farm. Cynthia, her older daughter, also was 32 and supposedly had received Barney as a birthday present when she was two from her father, Gerald Wharton, who had died a few years ago.

Cynthia had learned to ride on Barney. Claudia, her younger sister, also had learned on his gentle, safe back. Both girls went on to bigger, fancier mounts over the years, but Barney's usefulness remained. He was trained to pull a cart and appeared in the local annual Christmas parade; in fact, he had not missed a parade for almost 25 years.

Rufe's three kids had learned their early horsemanship with Barney—as had Whitey's son. Barney also introduced Cynthia's two children, now eight and five, and Claudia's six-year-old to riding. A few years ago, when my five-year-old daughter, Janie, had shown an interest in having a horse, I took her to Woodhill several times to ride Barney. We saddled him up—he was probably 24 then—put her on his back, and turned them loose in a paddock. As long as he felt Janie's weight on his back, Barney walked quietly and slowly. If he did not feel her weight; if Janie overadjusted as he made a turn, he stopped. If she fell, he stopped.

Barney's usefulness was not limited to children. He was the best equine babysitter I have ever seen. You could put him with the wildest weanlings in the world and somehow he became their friend and surrogate. To catch even the most contrary babies, all that was necessary was to call Barney.

"Hey, Barney!" He would stop what he was doing and start slowly across the field toward the caller. Somehow he knew he was not the only one wanted; he would stop and check out the where-abouts of his charges, and if they were not following he went back to them and let them know they were to follow. And they did.

Occasionally, Woodhill received a layup off the track, and Barney would be the horse's attendant until the animal settled down. He also helped calm recently retired fillies, and I do not recall Woodhill ever having a filly with a letdown problem, which I frequently saw everywhere else. The only apparent difference was Barney.

He was invaluable when trying to load balky horses. He went anywhere you led him—into any kind of van or trailer—and more often than not other horses followed him. Anyone who ever had a skittish yearling to ship had to appreciate that.

But old Barney had not taken this last winter well. He had begun to look his age. He moved slower and his old backbone sagged. Whitey said he was not getting around well, and his eyesight was suspect.

Whitey pulled a slip of paper out of his pocket and handed it to me. I read it: "Dr. Kelley, Please put Barney to sleep. I think his time has come. Estelle Wharton."

"I hate this, Whitey," I said as I tucked the note into my pocket. "This is probably the sweetest horse that ever lived."

"I know, Doc," Whitey said. "That's why Rufe ain't here. He's had that note the last two or three times you've been here and he keeps saying he forgot. Mrs. Wharton insisted today."

"What are you gonna do with Barney?" I asked.

"We'll bury him out back," Whitey answered. "A hole's already been dug."

"How are you gonna get him back there?"

"The wagon's hooked up to the tractor out back."

"Whitey, he weighs six hundred pounds," I said. "You'll never get him up on that thing."

"We're way ahead of you, Doc," Whitey said. "Take a look."

I walked out the rear of the barn and there was the tractor and flatbed wagon. Leaning against the wagon were four or five long 2 x 12s, forming a ramp at about a 30-degree angle from the ground.

"We'll walk him right up there," Whitey said. "He'll go anywhere you lead him."

"I guess there's nothing to do but get on with it, then," I said. "Go ahead and get him on the wagon. I'll get the stuff."

James, the kid who worked in Barn 3, put a shank on Barney and took him out of his stall as I went back to my car. On my list of favorite things, euthanizing anything comes just below having my teeth pulled with pliers.

I took the bottle of euthanasia solution from my trunk and got a needle and syringe. I drew enough for a 600-pound horse into the syringe and noticed there was only a small amount left in the vial, not enough for another horse, so I pulled it into the syringe, too. I looked at the amount and saw it was about a 750 or 800 pound dose. With normal medications, I am careful to use the correct dosages, but I did not feel an overdose was particularly dangerous to this patient. Overkill was not a worry.

I went out behind the barn and Barney and James were on the wagon. As I walked up the ramp, I noticed Whitey's eyes were a little moist. He saw me looking and turned away. "I'll go get the tractor keys." he said. "You go ahead." And he walked into the barn.

"The keys are in the tractor," James whispered after Whitey left. I patted Barney's head a couple of times. "Old boy, I'm sorry, but I guess it's necessary," I told him as I choked up a little, too.

The injection was quick. Barney went down almost before I could get the needle out of the vein. I waited a couple of minutes and checked the palpebral reflex. None. He was gone.

Whitey came back out. He spoke to James. "Pull his halter. Mrs. Wharton wants it." Then to me "Rufe needs you over at the mare barn." He acted angry.

I drove over to Barn 2. Rufus did not mention Barney or ask how things went. We solemnly went through the mares. It was April, the middle of the breeding season, and checking mares was what I did most. One mare had lost her foal after a dystocia and had developed a nasty mastitis. She took quite a while to examine and we were probably at Barn 2 for 45 minutes. Rufus never once mentioned Barney.

After finishing, I put things back in my car and reviewed the follicles of several mares with Rufus. Whitey and James drove by on the tractor, heading to the rear of the farm. They should have dumped their load by now, I thought, instead of just heading back with it.

Rufus stopped talking and stared at the wagon with its unhappy cargo. I could see the tears forming. "Doc, I never felt so bad about anything in my life," he said.

The wagon was about 50 feet past us. I started to agree with Rufus, but before I could speak, Barney lifted his head.

This was not possible! I had given Barney a 20% to 30% overdose of the most potent euthanasia solution available. I had checked his palpebral reflex. He was dead!

"Stop!" I shouted and ran toward the wagon as Whitey put on the brakes. Rufus was right behind me.

I hopped up next to Barney as he rolled up on his belly. He looked over at me and gave a very drunken nicker.

"Rufe, he's alive!" I yelled.

For the first time since I had been on the farm that day, Rufus smiled. "I'm no vet, Doc," he beamed, "but I think you're right!"

The old pony struggled to get to his feet. Rufus told Whitey to pull the wagon over to the loading chute. Barney's halter was gone, so Rufus looped the shank he was holding around Barney's neck, and guided him gently off the wagon. He staggered badly.

"Doc, I ain't gonna let you do this again." Rufus said. Whitey and James smiled as broadly as he did.

If they had headed straight back with the wagon when I had left Barn 3, Barney would have been in the hole and covered up by now. They explained that the tractor did not want to start and they had to call Willie, the farm mechanic, to get it going.

"Is Mrs. Wharton in the house?" I asked. They said, yes, so I told them to put Barney back in his stall. I was not about to try again.

I drove back to the house. A couple of extra cars were there, but company or not, I needed to speak to Mrs. Wharton. She answered the door with red eyes and handkerchief in hand. Behind her were her daughters, Cynthia and Claudia, with tears streaming down their faces. Barney's demise had brought them together to share the unhappy time.

"Is it over, Dr. Kelley?" Mrs. Wharton asked.

I told her what had happened. I do not recall ever making three women so happy.

That was a few years ago. Barney still did not get around too well. He did not winter too well and spent a lot of time inside in cold weather. He bumped into things sometimes, so he shared a small, treeless, paddock, with a quiet, old ex-racehorse gelding as a buddy.

I asked other veterinarians if they had ever had a euthanasia failure. None had. I checked to make sure I had not accidentally used a bottle of solution that had expired, but it was still well within date. I called the drug company and asked if anyone ever had reported a problem. No one had, but I was told that perhaps the vial had become contaminated from a previous use, thereby reducing its effectiveness. I do not believe that was the case, but I cannot say for sure. All I know is that Barney did not stay dead that April day several years ago.

Barney lived four more years before he died peacefully in his sleep.

⟶ Willie of the Winds

A woolly Shetland pony stood chained to a tree, desperately in need of some groceries. Anne Sikorski spotted him as she drove by. She realized she had to act fast. She parked her car at home and returned to the pony.

She didn't bother with pleasantries: this pony was starving. Freeing him from the tree, she walked him home.

Her vet, Dr. Frank Palka, shook his head when he looked at the pony. He didn't think he would make it. The tiny thing was merely skin and bones.

But Anne, and Willie, refused to give up. Anne patiently nursed him back to health. She would feed the little guy small bits of grain dozens of times a day. As his condition improved she realized how pretty he was, and that he was truly a pony of a different color. His grayish roan coloring came chrome-plated, with a white mane, tail, blaze, and socks.

Anne's daughter JoAnn Gross was grown and had no kids of her own yet, so Anne didn't have a need for a small pony. Once Willie regained his health, she sold him to a family in nearby East Haddam. The daughter rode Willie everywhere and tried everything with him. The two could be seen going up and down local roads, showing in both Western and English tack, and tearing across fields in hunter paces.

Willie became so beloved by his family that when a hurricane threatened the area, they took Willie into the house, keeping him in the kitchen for safety.

When the daughter outgrew him, Willie was sold to another family, and then others, as kids outgrew him. In each home Willie taught more kids to ride and show. Willie could also drive, and he would face every obstacle in a trail class without hesitation. He never let anything rattle him. There was nothing the pony couldn't do.

There was also nothing the pony wouldn't eat. Well, except asparagus. Cherry jello, French fries (pile on the ketchup!) with orange soda, peanut butter and jelly sandwiches: all were on his menu.

Things changed when JoAnn's daughter Stephanie was born. When Stephanie was five, old enough to ride, JoAnn decided it was time to have Willie back in the family.

Willie's presence at the farm changed the herd dynamics immediately. There was no question who ruled the roost. No one messed with Willie.

JoAnn had never been able to convince her huge, traditional style Quarter Horse Barley to leave the driveway. But with Willie around it was no longer a problem. Willie became Barley's leader: Barley would follow him anywhere. If Willie went in the trailer, Barley would go in the trailer. If Barley was going to a show, Willie had better be going as well. Because without Willie, Barley was not going.

Willie's tiny size and Barley's build, which towered over him, made the pair look like Mutt and Jeff.

Stephanie learned to ride on Willie. He also enjoyed playing games with her.

Stephanie would tell her mom, "I want to go riding."

JoAnn, busy, would answer, "I'm making dinner," or "I'm cleaning." But she would add, "If you can catch that little pony, you can ride him."

Stephanie would catch Willie, groom him, and tack him

up. Soon JoAnn would see her ride by the window.

Thirty seconds later, Willie would be back. Minus Stephanie.

A short time would elapse and Stephanie would come stomping in, furious that the pony had once again dumped her.

Stephanie was not allowed to ride until her mother got home from work. So when she got out of school, she would head to the barn and read to Willie and the other horses until JoAnn got home. It was a foreshadowing of Stephanie's future career as a teacher.

When Stephanie rode Willie in the grass ring at home, Willie felt that the grass riding surface served a dual purpose. As they trotted or cantered, he would drop his head to snatch some grass, and off Stephanie would pop, right over his head. Since it was such a short distance to the ground, Stephanie would emerge unhurt. Sometimes she and JoAnn laughed at Willie's antics until their sides hurt.

Stephanie took excellent care of her pony: grooming, wrapping him, and of course hugging him. By the time she was six, Stephanie could wrap Willie, lead him to the trailer, and load him. Willie certainly had his own opinions about things, but he had a lot of patience for a pony. He even dealt with Stephanie's passion for purple, resignedly putting up with a purple halter, purple wraps, a purple saddle pad, and being brushed with purple brushes.

In their first show together, Willie and Stephanie got stuck between a big horse and the rail. The judge had to lean down just to see the tiny pony hidden behind the horse. Willie and Stephanie got a third. It was the lowest ribbon they would ever receive.

Willie behaved beautifully in a show ring, much better than he did at home. He knew he had a job to do, and he loved it. Just as he had with the family before, he took perfect care of Stephanie at the horse shows. He was always dependable. The trophies and championships Stephanie won on the pony can be found throughout much of the house. The picture the pint-sized pony and his adorable little rider made proved irresistible to judges.

Willie's favorite after-show snack was French fries with lots of ketchup, and orange soda. As much as he might want his beloved combo during the show, he had to wait until the end of the day. The white of his wide blaze dyed in red and orange just wouldn't be the right look for the show ring.

After his snack, he enjoyed swimming in a lake located near one of the show venues that the Grosses frequented.

At a horse show any child could ride Willie: he would never take a wrong step. At home, however, he continued to be a pony. Willie had a finely honed skill for getting loose, and when he did, no one could catch him. The pony would run the family ragged, chasing him hither and yon. Once he had had his fun with them, Willie would suddenly decide he'd had enough, and in he would come. Then he would put on his innocent face, and look at the family as if to say, "Was there a problem?"

One day JoAnn, thanks to a broken ankle, was unable to feed. Stephanie went to the barn to feed in the pouring rain. Willie seized the opportunity to escape and flew out into the muddy barnyard. JoAnn's nephew Raymond happened to be visiting and tried to help out. As Willie flew by, Raymond caught him, wrapping his arms around Willie's neck. It didn't even slow Willie down. The pony just kept going, with Raymond along for the ride, skiing through the mud.

Another time the Grosses were building an addition to the barn. Willie, getting into trouble as always, had been kicked in the face and developed an infection. He was turned out in the round pen by himself while JoAnn and Stephanie nursed his injury. The injury did not prevent him from playing bratty pony tricks. When JoAnn took him out of the round pen (to put him back in the barn), Willie broke loose and took off.

A four foot deep ditch had been dug in anticipation of the addition and a cement wall rose out of it, with metal posts sticking up through the wall. Willie, naturally, headed right for it. JoAnn held her breath as Willie attempted to jump the ditch. He didn't make it. He crashed into it, cement and metal posts and all.

No one wanted to look. JoAnn was sure he was dead after such a disastrous crash. But Willie definitely had some feline branches in his family tree. He'd already used up several lives, and there went another. The pony was fine.

Some of JoAnn's happiest memories are of the trail rides she and Stephanie took together. While JoAnn trotted along on Barley, Willie would gallop furiously to keep up. It was wonderful to hear Stephanie's laughter, to know how much she enjoyed riding, and life. And she and Willie were so darn cute together!

JoAnn's son Michael and his wife Katie recently had their first child: a daughter named Angelica. At a tender age, Angelica was placed on Willie's back for pony rides. Willie, as always, proved perfectly dependable, aware that he was responsible for this precious little life.

Willie's life with the Sikorskis and Grosses spanned an amazing four generations, from Anne, to her granddaughter Stephanie, to her great-granddaughter Angelica.

Stephanie says he was "the best pony you could ask for, because he was fresh, but he also taught you and he took care of you." Willie knew when he could test a rider, and when he had to be good and take care of a rider. Although Stephanie gives all the credit to Willie, her father Ron says that Stephanie and JoAnn are in large part responsible for who Willie was. Ron says proudly that they are both so calm around horses, "they work magic with them."

Willie was into his forties when he died. The spunky pony who taught so many kids in Connecticut how to show is buried behind JoAnn and Ron's house with a plaque above the grave in Willie's honor. JoAnn's mother Anne was buried with a lock of Willie's mane.

⤳ Bubbilicious

(An essay written by McKenzie Redfern)
McKenzie's assigned topic (in her mind, "the best ever") was—
Describe a lesson or a horse show from your horse's point of view.

Today is another day at Fox Hill Farms where I live. Let me introduce myself, my name is Bubbilicious. I am a chestnut Shetland pony (But I know, I am a true Red Head, and guess what? my mane has a pink glow!) I may be small in height and a little round in the girth, but I have a large personality. McKenzie Redfern is my rider and friend. She takes really good care of me, and in turn, I love taking care of her. I just love it when she brings me the special apple treats she makes, and she knows the special places to rub and scratch me between my ears. She is funny, kind and understands me, and is like a younger sister, but not as cute as I am!

I have heard the trainers say I am very good with children, especially in the Walk Trot, and I feel very special to be allowed to work with the children in the Pegasus program. Now, when it comes to jumping and the Short Stirrup, I have heard I can be a little naughty and sometimes quite stubborn, which I admit to, but I can't think why they call me temperamental when really all I want to do is have fun. As everyone knows, there are some jumps I like, and some jumps I don't! As far as I am concerned, I am lovable, cuddly and very cute.

Whoa woo wow, why I am I in these itchy braids? And what's in my tail? Oh no, there's a braid in my tail! Ok, maybe they can mess with my forelock, but they cannot "Mess with the tail!" They are going just too far this time. You know, the last time "the red forelock" was braided, it came out, and it was most embarrassing, and I looked just like Elvis!

"Hey Spotlight, Tic –Tac" (my two best friends) "are you both braided too?"

"Ya, we're braided."

"Hey girls it's truck time, that means food time!"

"Now Spot, don't be hogging the hay, my neck may be short but I can still nibble at your knees if you don't share."

It was not a long ride on the truck today, not even enough time to eat all the hay. But my trainer Alaina must have thought I had, because boy, did she give me a work out this morning, I'm all sweaty. Back to the truck for a rub down, and maybe I will force myself to have a little "pick me up" of hay, before they put the bridle back on. Not enough time, I got a nice rub down, but no more hay, McKenzie's coming. I should watch my waistline anyway, but I may hit the "Salad bar" of luscious green grass when I'm in the ring.

We're both clean as a whistle and groomed to be proud and now we are going through the list: clean show pad, check. Clean saddle and stirrups, check. Clean bit and I like the taste, check. Oiled hooves, check. Do we need the martingale? Check. Rider here, check. Hat, gloves and number, check. Crop ugh, I can't see one, but then she never lets me see she has one, I wonder if it's behind her back?

I think my braids look nicer than McKenzie's but her bows are fun. Now the part I don't like, the tightening of the girth! I really have to suck my tummy in. The stirrups are level and we are ready to go. I hope they do the flat first, I really have to work my way up to the jumping part. I still get scared, as I have not been jumping very long and definitely not at many shows. But McKenzie and I are a team, and I know when she moved up to Short Stirrup this year I wanted to move up with her as well. It was a bit bumpy at the beginning, as we were both green, and had a lot to learn together.

The trainers Alaina, Ruth and Joanna are patient, caring and really knowledgeable and don't let either of us get away with anything. Now, there have been times I should have dumped McKenzie on the floor, especially in last week's class when she did that tight turn, and if it had been anyone else I would have watched them sail in the air! But, I remember how McKenzie helped me at the last show when I was so scared of the man standing by the jump.

Okay, "It's Show Time." The martingale is staying on, oh panic attack, that means the jumping is first. Alaina is talking to McKenzie, what does she mean she has to be as brave as a pirate? Oh no, I see flowers! I don't jump flowers, I eat flowers. Help we're about to go in, but no one is telling the judge that Bubbles does *not* jump flowers. Spotlight and Tic-Tac seemed to be ok about the flowers, maybe they have not seen them yet. Okay, McKenzie, we're a team, I'm really, really scared, but if you think we can jump flowers today, we will jump flowers today.

McKenzie is whispering in my ear. "It's okay don't be scared, c'mon Bubbles, we can do this, one jump at a time." She tells me it's just another challenge we have to get through, and that it's not about what place we come today, it's about overcoming our fears. I wonder if she will let me do it with my eyes closed. But then I would not want McKenzie to do that, would I? We're in the ring, we have the right diagonal and we're posting nicely, and trying not to think about flowers. For the first time in my life I am not even hungry! We have picked up the canter and we are on the right lead. Okay we are going for it.

Oh my gosh, I hope she's feeling confident and looking up, and not at the those big yellow flowers. We're over the first jump, six steps and another jump, and she did not get up my neck. I feel McKenzie thinks we're going to be fine. She's looking at the next jump, I see red flowers, I'm really scared, I hope McKenzie will help me through this, she seems to know what she is doing. Now the yellow flowers back again, hang on, I know what they are trying to do is scare me. Well I am Bubbilicious, brave as a pirate and we can do anything if we work as a team. I am feeling a little more confident, and McKenzie and I are over the last jump.

McKenzie is giving me a big hug, a lot of pats. Alaina is smiling and saying "Awesome." We were a little fast, but it sounds good to me as I was out of the ring quicker.

Okay, I will slow it down a little for the next one. Now it's our turn to go back in the ring. This trip is nowhere near as bad as the first one, and I did not stop to smell the flowers, and we even got the lead changes. I see the possibility of treats ahead. The flat classes went very well. I did have a slight problem at the halt, because I really wanted to nibble the grass on the side. But I felt so proud of myself from the jumping, I pretended I was 14 hands tall and a fancy show pony, and I felt like I was walking on air as I pranced around the ring with my ears forward.

McKenzie and I worked very hard today to overcome my flower fear. I trusted her completely in the way she rode and the way she acted. I heard her thanking her trainers for everything they had taught her and because they had confidence in her, she had confidence in herself. That was our win today.

But now it's time to go back to the truck and see where my friends are, and a little R and R, and a whole lot of hay, that is if Spotlight has not eaten it first.

The End

McKenzie submitted this essay for the JACK ROCKWELL AWARD of the Fairfield Westchester Professional Horseman's Association.

HORSE TERMS AND TIPS

Horse Terms

Hock: Financial condition of all horse owners

Fence: Decorative structure built to provide your horse with something to chew on

Horse Auction: What you think of having after your horse bucks you off

Pinto: Green coat pattern found on freshly washed light colored horses left unattended for two minutes

Rasp: Abrasive metal tool used to remove excess skin from ones' knuckles

Lunging: Popular training method in which a horse exercises their owner by spinning them in circles until dizzy

Easy to Catch: In a 10 x 10 stall

Hives: What you get when you receive the vet bill for your six horses, three dogs and four cats

Hobbles: Walking gait of a horse owner after their foot has been stepped on by their horse

Dog House: What you are in when you spend too much money on grooming supplies and pretty halters

Important Things for Horse Owners to Know

If you want your mare to go into labor, take a nap

Want it to rain? Mow a field of hay

Important Things for Blonde Horse Owners to Know

Be sure to check the bed of your pickup truck for hay and grain *before* you go through the car wash

The judge does not award extra points for designing your own course

When loading your trailer to go to the horse show, remember to load the horse, too

Idis

Monday Morning
Photo by James L. Parker

Pasha

Photo by Alice Henshaw

Matt Mills and Easy Otie Whiz
at the 2006 World Equestrian Games
in Aachen, Germany

Bob Langrish Photo

*An undefeated Barbaro captures
the Kentucky Derby*

Photo credit CindyDulay/Horse-Races.net

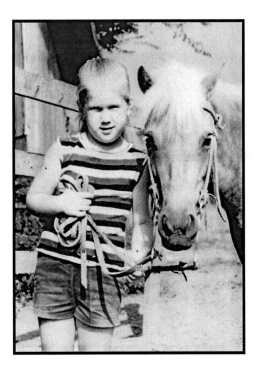

Sugar and Elizabeth

Tip

Photo: Brian Wilcox/Connecticutphoto

Count on Me
at Gladstone
Photo: Bruce H. Scarborough of BHS Photography

Jabberwocky and Anna Vaculik
at King Oak Horse Trials
2009
Hoof Pix® Sport Horse Photography

Harrison

Spike and Zane

Blue Hors Matine
and Andreas Helgstrand

Photos: Diana De Rosa

116

Theodore O'Connor
and Karen O'Connor

Photos: Diana De Rosa

117

Rebel
one of 163 horses saved from
Sugarcreek Kill Auction, is now a very
successful barrel racer.

Bubblicious and McKenzie
tackle the scary flowers
at Gardnertowm Farm in Newburgh, NY

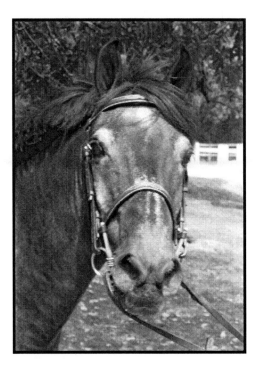

Dazzle

Striker and Nikole Ruddy
Killington, VT 1991
Childrens Jumper Class

Sarge

Willie and Steph

Rex

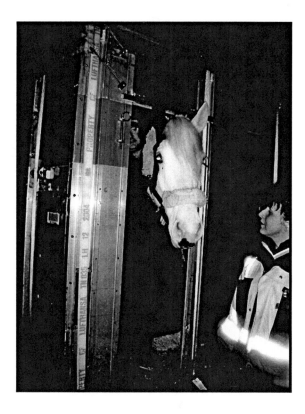

Kells leaving for Germany

Helium and Anne Moss
competing at Devon

My Thriller

Fred Astaire (Tucker)

Deb Persson photo

Twin Pond Disco Kid
competing at an NRHA Competition
at the Ohio State Fair Grounds

Waldenberry Photo

Renee Luther (behind the horse)
teaching a lesson at Freedom Hills. The new
indoor and house are in the background.

SURPRISES

⤳ A Brush with Royalty

Hope Hand doesn't know how the event managed to go on. The weather in Great Britain was unreal. Torrential rains had flooded the roads, made seas of mud out of fields, and stranded people in cars and trains, as well as in their homes. In some areas more than a month's worth of rain had fallen in 24 hours. Several towns reported the highest rainfall on record.

The rain resulted in the biggest rescue effort in peacetime history. Hope was right in the middle of it. As a member of the Jury of Appeals of the Federation Equestre Internationale Technical Committee, she had come to Hartpury College in England to represent the United States for the World Para Dressage Championships. (In 2006 the Paraequestrian events had become the eighth discipline of the FEI.)

Hope's job is to oversee any protests, and make a ruling after hearing the facts. Protests happen frequently at these events, considering the subjectivity of dressage judging. As committee members have to be prepared for all types of issues, there are frequent meetings. One of the purposes of the meetings is to go over proposed rules, with the goal of constantly improving the process.

Officials and judges came from all over the world. Some were trapped at the venue, where they had to stay in the college dorms without a change of clothes. Grooms were kicked out of the dorm and slept on floors wherever they could find space. Although Hope was unable to get back to the bed and breakfast she had been scheduled to stay in, she had managed to find substitute accommodations which were just fine: sleeping with the barn dogs on a couch in a house right at the venue.

When Hope and the other officials finally were able to make their way back to the hotel, they saw desperate people with horses, cows, and sheep in tow behind their belongings in waist high waters. People were lined along the roads, trapped in their cars with their kids and dogs, waiting for help.

The previous year, the FEI had elected a new President, Princess Haya of Jordan. The Princess had competed internationally since the age of 13 and participated in the 2000 Olympics in Sydney and the 2002 World Equestrian Games. She captured the Presidency in a heated battle.

It didn't matter what the weather was, Hope had to do her job. That required her to be in the thick of it. And she was, sitting in her wheelchair in the pouring rain. Those in wheelchairs were towed to their sites through the mud by golf carts. Hope had to travel the large expanse of the college, from one arena to the other, up and down grades behind a golf cart.

Despite the weather, the competitors and show organizers all did their best. No one complained. Instead they all pitched in and did the best they could while maintaining a positive attitude. Hope has been an IRS agent for 41 years, starting at the age of 17. She has traveled the world. IRS agents learn a lot about people. She was impressed with everyone at the event and commended them all for their determination to see it through.

No stranger to competition herself, Hope was team captain in 2000 at the Sydney Olympics for the Para Dressage Team, where she finished sixth, and took a Reserve in Atlanta. She took Gold in the British Invitational event. The events were made tougher by the fact that Paraequestrians generally have to catch ride. They had one week not only to get to know their horse, but to learn a musical freestyle! (Since Sydney, however, the competition has changed, and riders now compete on their own horses, raising the bar and resulting in some magnificent horse and rider combinations and incredible competition!)

As Hope sat at Hartpury, the wheels of her chair half buried in mud, a petite, pretty young woman came up to her. She told Hope that they would be handing out the awards together. Hope looked at her in amazement. Crisp, clean, and neatly dressed, the woman showed no trace of the mud that coated everyone and everything else. Mystified by the immaculate state of the newcomer, Hope asked how she had arrived.

"I flew in in a helicopter," the woman answered.

"A helicopter!" exclaimed Hope. "Well, isn't that nice!" She couldn't help the sarcasm that snuck into her voice. Here Hope was in her wheelchair in the mud, being towed around by golf carts, and this young lady had flown in by helicopter! Where was the justice in that?

Shortly afterwards they moved to the indoor to hand out the awards. The young woman went to the podium, where she was introduced. Hope's new friend was none other than Princess Haya.

Hope did a double take. Whoops. She might not have taken quite that tone of voice had she known she was talking to the President of the FEI!

The Princess, known for her graciousness, had not taken the remark to heart. Looking straight at Hope, she winked.

⌒⁀⋅⟩ SARGE

Sarge came to Elaine and her sister Joyce in trade for a registered Arabian gelding. The 14.3 hand Quarter/Morgan cross was a mess. His rough, filthy coat covered protruding bones and a sagging back. His feet were cracked and broken due to lack of care, and his lower lip "hung so low, it was a miracle he didn't catch it when he walked."

Although the dealer told them he was 12 years old, his teeth told the real story. Sarge was closer to 28. Elaine traded in a $2500 Arabian for a horse worth a slaughterhouse price. She would never have guessed at the time, but it was a horse that turned out to be a gift from God.

The Arab had been purchased for Joyce against Elaine's better judgment. Elaine's instinct proved correct when, only a week later, she found herself with a horse her rookie sister couldn't handle. It was out of sheer desperation that Elaine traded the horse for Sarge, the only horse the dealer had available for trade.

Sarge had four brands on him, attesting to his career as a United States Government border patrol horse. In a later career, he was trained to barrel race. When Elaine took Sarge on a test drive in the meadow behind their home, that training created a real problem. Sarge became highly agitated in the open field, ready to run.

Elaine had a neighbor, an experienced Western trainer, try him. The trainer said Sarge was "scary," a real loose cannon. If she merely touched him with a knee on either side of the saddle he would jump sideways. Definitely not suited for a beginner rider like Joyce, Elaine decided. In fact, not suited for anyone to ride in an open field. Sarge was looking for the barrels!

Yet she hated to send him back to the dealer. It was quite clear what his fate would be should he return. She decided to give him one more chance. Maybe he would be different on a trail.

Although she planned to try him the next day, Sarge had other plans. He got loose and ran down a paved road. Then he veered onto a gravel driveway, ending up in a neighbor's backyard.

It was Joyce who caught him. On the long walk back home, she and Sarge bonded. As they walked, Joyce gently explained the rules of horse behavior to Sarge. Running loose in the road was not acceptable. Something clicked in Sarge as he realized he had found a friend.

From that moment on, the dead look in Sarge's eyes started to fade. He had made the choice that Joyce was his rider, his person. No one but Joyce was allowed on his back. The few times Elaine tried riding him he made it clear he wanted no part of her. He would immediately dance around, crow hop, and back into ditches.

For Joyce, the story was entirely different. He turned out to be an excellent trail horse: a real babysitter. If he lost his balance on slippery footing, he would scramble to keep her in the saddle. One time she tried to mount and just couldn't quite get up on him. Sarge leaned into her and lowered his neck to help her make it into the saddle.

He had great patience with Joyce. She never could remember how to tack up correctly. He would stand quietly while she fumbled putting on his bridle. Sarge would glance over at Elaine, his bridle hanging askew, and let out a mighty sigh. The look on his face, says Elaine, "was priceless."

Sarge seemed to read Joyce's mind: he was always impeccably tuned in to her. His ears would flick back and forth while she rode him, assessing her mood minute by minute. If she were upset, he would be the perfect ride, taking not a step out of place. If she were in high spirits, he would match her with his own brand of high jinks: tail flagging, neck arched, prancing down the road with all the brio of a youngster.

Over the next two years, his back became strong and level, his weight returned to normal, his lip firmed, and his coat shone. He became a beautiful liver chestnut with a flaxen mane and tail and a sparkle in his eyes. For a horse his age, his stamina was incredible, and he had the cleanest legs of any horse Elaine had ever known.

Eventually, Sarge forgot the barrels, and enjoyed galloping across open meadows. He even won ribbons at some local hunter paces.

Sarge came to Elaine and Joyce in pitiable shape, without a friend anywhere. They gave him a loving home with the best of feed and care, the freedom to come and go out of his stall as he pleased, and buddies to keep him company.

Although he was the last horse Elaine would have wanted in the trade, he turned out to be the best horse she could have received. He was, she says, "an angel in horse clothing."

WORKING HORSES

↬ Black Jack

For a public grieving its fallen commander, the vision of the riderless horse said it all. And the horse knew, knew he had a role of immense importance to play that somber November afternoon. His proud carriage, his elegant movement, told the world how completely he understood the assignment.

John Fitzgerald Kennedy, the youngest and 35th president of the United States, was dead, ambushed by bullets the source of which the world may never know. The United States mourned, the world mourned, this inspirational man who had proven such a source of hope for his country. The nation was dumbstruck by his death.

The horse was solid black, a sixteen-year-old Quarter Horse/Morgan cross. The boots placed in his saddle faced backwards, representing the slain leader, as he trotted up Seventeenth Street.

When Black Jack was selected for the funeral procession, First Lady Jackie Kennedy was unaware of the horse's name. When she learned of it, she was amazed. Her father had regularly been addressed by the nickname Black Jack.

Black Jack—the horse—became a hero and a symbol for the nation. The horse's comportment during President Kennedy's funeral caused him to be selected for the funerals of Dwight D. Eisenhower, Herbert Hoover, Lyndon Johnson, and General Douglas MacArthur.

His fame brought Black Jack scores of visitors. Unlike most

horses, who interact only with horse lovers, Black Jack's highly visible role caused him to be seen and remembered by the entire nation. On his 29th birthday, 1500 guests attended his party, and a fan brought him a butter pecan cake weighing nearly 200 pounds.

When he was humanely put down after 24 years of distinguished service, a full military funeral followed. Black Jack was buried in Virginia on the Fort Myer parade ground, Summerall Field.

Black Jack's stall still remains as a shrine.

⤳ Police Horse

He was a comedian, always looking for a laugh. He patrolled a busy, bustling intersection: Lefferts Boulevard and Liberty Avenue in the Richmond Hill section of Queens, New York. Buses, cars, and trains, all traversed it. The imposing bay horse and the policeman were always there, always keeping an eye on what was happening.

People were used to seeing them patrolling that corner of the neighborhood. Locals and tourists alike would come up to pet the horse, talk to his rider, and perhaps take a photo of them.

The cop may have been serious about his job, but his horse wasn't. When a visiting couple stopped to take his photo, the officer stood next to his horse's side, providing a photo opportunity of a beautiful horse and a handsome cop. Just as the couple went to snap the shot, the horse threw his head to the side, sending the cop sprawling onto the hood of an adjacent car.

Girls were forever attracted to the good-looking young policeman. While he was busy flirting with the pretty ones, his horse was only too willing to help. He would nuzzle into pocketbooks, coming out with wallets, compacts, and other interesting objects.

Margaret Bjork, a born animal lover, would always pet the horse and was one of the people who brought him goodies. She thought the horse was spectacular: so big she could almost have walked under his belly, gorgeous with his shiny cocoa brown coat and black mane and tail, and heroic with the big scar across his leg that he had garnered during his tour of duty.

Margaret worked in a nearby shoe store. On her breaks she would go to the Korean Grocer for fruits and vegetables, and come out with carrots with their tops still attached, a treat she knew the horse loved.

She was very faithful about bringing him goodies. Every week she would cash her paycheck, get her groceries, and buy the horse his carrots. Every week he would wait expectantly for his treats.

But one week, Margaret was too busy. She didn't have time to go shopping; she had to go straight to her job in the shoe store. The temperature that day soared, and the shoe store soon became stifling. In the hope of some relief, the doors were left open to catch any possible breezes from outside.

The horse meanwhile was missing his carrots. He decided that, since they had not come to him, he was just going to have to go looking for them.

Margaret was working when she heard a customer scream in terror. Looking up, she saw the huge horse in the doorway, his head, neck, and shoulders inside the store. He had squeezed in as far as he possibly could. "Where were those carrots?" Margaret laughed, and then soothed the terrified customer.

After that, the carrots always arrived as scheduled.

.

GARTH (AKA HARRISON)

Okay, so his vocals would not sell millions of CDs, but his eyes and his big bottom lip would melt anyone's heart. He was a pack mule for Phantom Ranch, working the Grand Canyon. Garth worked hard, hauling anything and everything into and out of the canyon. The sacks he carried on his strong back might contain mail or tools or toilet paper. In the summer the temperatures can reach 115 degrees so Garth was one tough hombre.

One day the wrangler from Phantom Ranch went out to the corral to get the mules ready and found the big Percheron mule down. Garth's injury was serious: he had a broken hip. It looked like the end of the road for the hard working guy.

That was when Garth's first piece of luck kicked in. Instead of being put down, Garth went to a man who turned him out to pasture for a year to see if he could heal. He didn't improve, so once again it looked like the end was near: he was headed to the auction. But lady luck smiled once more for Garth, and a couple who had seen him asked if they could take him instead. He spent a month with them before coming to Best Friends Animal Society in Kanab, Utah.

Best Friends is a unique shelter located in the stunning Red Rock area of Utah. It houses over 2000 animals, from horses and cats and dogs to pigs, bunnies, and birds. For animals who are not adoptable, Best Friends provides a safe haven for the rest of their lives, where nothing bad will ever happen to them again.

When the Best Friends vet, Dr. Tara, initially looked at Garth, it was clear that his hip had been broken, most likely from being kicked while in the corrals with the other mules. He certainly had a hitch in his get-a-long, however it seemed to be more of a mechanical lameness than a painful lameness. There wasn't much to be done about the injury, but he was wormed, and had his teeth floated and feet trimmed. The best part of the deal was when everyone told him how handsome he was!

Garth stands about 15 hands and is a big boned, heavy dark bay, with a big head, and the "cutest big bottom lip." It looks, says Jen Reid of Best Friends, "like a big square shovel." Light brown frames his eyes and lips.

Garth was very nice to be around and the entire staff fell in love with the gentle old guy. Although he wasn't the sort to rush over and ask for loving, (being much more reserved than that), with some time and patience his personality started to creep out.

As Jen says, "He's actually quite a delicate little soul for such a big strong mule. Mules may seem tough and stubborn but are actually often very sensitive and emotional."

Garth's luck continued to hold, and at Best Friends he found a wonderful new adoptive home. Dan and Jares Gallagher were working at the sanctuary at the time and had recently lost one of their older horses, April, to Cushing's disease. Their remaining horse Annie (a mustang who adopted them) was lonely and needed a friend. Dan and Jares wanted someone who was gentle and quiet and would be a good companion for Annie. Garth seemed like a perfect match.

The Gallagher's corral is relatively flat and not too large: a perfect space for Garth with his injury. Annie is submissive so they knew she wouldn't push Garth around and hurt his bad leg. When Garth came to the Gallaghers for the "first date" with Annie, everyone agreed that it was a great fit. So it became official and Garth joined the Gallagher family.

Garth was renamed Harrison and now has a great new home keeping Annie (and the Gallaghers) happy. He gets pampered the way every working mule should be and is loved even though he can't work anymore. He gets the Sunday paper read to him. Dan gives him massages. Dan and Jares sit out in the sun with him, reading, or bring out cots and spend the night in the corral with their two big babies.

Jen says, "Dan and Jares are the most conscientious horse owners and wanted nothing more than someone to join their family and get lots of love."

He lives just up the road so Jen gets to visit him all the time. It's obvious to her how happy and content he is. And, just like proud parents, Dan and Jares will talk Jen's ear off about how great he is!

Since his adoption, Harrison's personality has bloomed. He's extremely smart and has learned to be an expert locksmith who can pick just about any lock. (Dan and Jares have learned they need to stay one step ahead of him!) Still a strong guy, he has definite ideas about the shape of his corral, and bulldozes the fence into whatever configuration suits his whim at the time.

Jares says, "I can't imagine life without him. We've both fallen head over heels in love with him." Although initially he was shy and unsure, especially with men, now he's calm and secure. Formerly he would accept petting and loving; now he actively solicits it.

Harrison has bonded so much with Annie that she follows him constantly. In fact, at times the Gallaghers have to put them in separate paddocks so that he can have a little down time.

Jares says unabashedly "I'm honored to pick up his manure because of what he's done; he's earned the right to be pampered!"

Although she has no riding horse right now, Jares is fine with it. She says, "Just being with Harrison and Annie is what's important."

For one smart mule, a well earned retirement is a sweet, sweet reward!

For more information, or to donate to Best Friends, call 435 644-2001, or check out the website at www.bestfriends.org.

⤳ School Bus

*R*esidents of Ryegate, Vermont became accustomed to an unusual sight in the early 1900's. A Standardbred horse named Rex would pass by many of their houses in the morning, and again in the late afternoon. Rex was delivering young Doris Gibson to the schoolhouse.

What made people do a double take was the fact that twice a day Rex walked by on his own, with no human in sight. He didn't just deliver Doris to the school. He dropped her off, went home unaided to the farm, and then returned on his own to pick her up when school let out.

Most of the neighborhood children walked to the schoolhouse, and Doris Gibson was no exception. She, her two sisters, and their brother made the trek five days a week. But the walk to the one-room schoolhouse nearly 100 years ago was not an easy one. It started downhill, but soon turned steeply uphill, and in cold or bad weather the hill seemed endless. School buses were non-existent; in fact, the first automobiles were just being built.

When first grader Doris was stricken with whooping cough, she was out of school, quarantined, for nearly a month. When it was time to return to school, the hill proved insurmountable. Doris was still coughing, and too weak to tackle it. An alternative method of getting to school had to be found.

Rex provided the solution. A former pacer at a racetrack located in St. Johnsbury, the bay gelding had been re-schooled to become the family's driving horse.

Rex didn't only drive; he had been schooled as a saddle horse as well. He was a great driving horse, and was used to pull the family buggy during warmer weather and the sleigh in the winter. His only downfall was that if he came across another team on the road, he was sure they were there for him to engage in a race!

So Rex was pressed into service to take Doris to school. There were no facilities for horses at the school, so Rex couldn't wait all day for Doris to finish her studies in order to take her home. But Rex proved very trainable. He seemed to understand the situation, and, with a little creativity and positive reinforcement, provided the perfect solution.

Doris's dad, Herbert Gibson, learned not to feed Rex his grain before they left for school. So Rex, wanting his breakfast, would come straight back home after dropping Doris off in order to get fed. Doris, meanwhile, learned to bring carrots and sugar cubes to school with her. In the afternoon her dad would saddle Rex, signaling the horse that it was time to pick up Doris. When he arrived at school, Rex would get his treats.

There was one temptation for Rex along the way. A neighboring farm, owned by the McLams, often had some hay spillage when they transferred the hay from where it was stored to the cow barn. Rex thought the dropped hay made a perfect snack. So Carlyle McLam stepped in, shooing Rex along his route when the horse tried to detour.

When Rex arrived at school, the older kids (the school housed all eight grades) would often help the little girl get on. Doris, who turned 101 in 2009, says "I never had trouble with what I wanted Rex to do; he just did it. We all expected him to do it and he did. Everything just worked out."

This smart and versatile horse was much more than the family driving and saddle horse. He had his route and timing down pat. Rex was the first school bus!

⟿ PASHA

The smallest dancing white stallion in the Big Apple Circus, Pasha stood only 14.2 hands. Descended from the elite Davenport Arabians, his exquisite dished face and liquid brown eyes (trainer Katia called him "Pony Bright Eyes") spoke of his intelligence and eagerness to please.

Pasha's life in the circus was a good one. Always well loved and well cared for, he enjoyed lush pastures when the circus was not in session and audience acclaim while performing.

Of course, there were the tough parts as well. Circus life required horses to live out of a trailer and spend much of their lives tied up, unable to move.

Because of his stature, Pasha was the one who had to do the tightest circles in the patterns the horses performed. In time, it became too much. The tiny circles took a toll on Pasha's back. He was sent away for rehabilitation to Double Star Ranch in Campbell Hall, New York, a farm owned by Darlene Williams and Vince Felty.

Dr. Allan Schoen, one of the top holistic vets in the country, performed his magic on Pasha. Pasha became sound again, but he didn't go back to the circus. Everyone reached the same conclusion: a return to the circus would only aggravate Pasha's back again.

But it wasn't such bad news. While caring for Pasha, Darlene had fallen in love with the pint-sized Arab. He remained at Double Star Ranch, while one of the ranch's horses went to the circus in his place.

Pasha's new career was much less intense than circus life. He went out on trails, learned dressage, and was ridden western. His small size made him perfect for the younger riders who composed most of Double Star's students.

In time, though, the younger riders grew up and on to bigger horses. Planning to move to Montana, Darlene and Vince didn't want to take on any new clients. Their good friend Nina ran nearby Whisper Wind Farm in Warwick, New York. Whisper Wind always was well populated with kids.

Darlene and Vince brought Pasha over for a trial. While there, Darlene had him demonstrate some of his circus tricks for Nina. Pasha performed on cue. He bowed, counted, reared, and walked on his hind legs.

Watching, Nina grew somewhat alarmed, especially when Pasha was walking on his hind legs. What if a little kid gave the wrong command and Pasha reared in response?

Aloud she said, "That can never happen during one of my lessons." The pony looked right at her.

A couple of days later, one of Nina's adult students took a dressage lesson on Pasha. It went well and afterwards the adult wanted to see Pasha do some of his tricks. Since there were no children around, Nina figured that would be all right.

The student gave Pasha the cue to do one of his tricks. The pony looked at Nina, and didn't move. The adult signaled him again. In fact, the adult tried asking Pasha several times, cueing him properly. The response was the same. Pasha did nothing. Again, he turned and looked at Nina.

Maybe he won't do them because I told him not to, Nina thought. "It's okay to do your tricks," she told the pony.

The adult repeated the cue. This time, Pasha responded.

The pony stayed.

Pasha became a great lesson pony, one all the kids loved to

ride. Yet there was a downside. Having performed as a stallion for much of his life, Pasha had been gelded late, when he became one of Double Star's horses. He retained some stallion-like traits, and those traits often got him into trouble in the paddock.

One day Nina discovered that Pasha's antics had gotten him kicked. Badly. His right front leg had sustained a spiral fracture. Dr. Janet Durso wasn't too sure about Pasha's prognosis. Recovery would mean a long period of remaining immobile. For the leg to heal, Pasha could not move for six to eight weeks. He could not take a step; he could not lie down.

Nina wasn't sure Pasha would cooperate, but she was sure she would give him the chance.

Pasha was confined in his stall, tied tightly. A strange thing happened. The pony took perfectly to his confinement. He didn't object; he didn't get cranky. He took it all in stride, remaining calm and quiet.

Two weeks later, Dr. Durso took a second set of x-rays. After viewing them, she asked Nina, "Do you want to hear the bad news or the good news?"

Always optimistic, Nina replied, "The good news."

"The break is healing well."

How could there be bad news, Nina thought, if the leg was healing well?

"So what's the bad news?" she asked.

"The break is much worse than we thought. The first set of x-rays wasn't that clear; this set shows just how bad a break we are dealing with."

That meant the lay up would be much longer than anticipated. Would Pasha be able to handle it?

He would. Pasha remained the perfect patient. He didn't need any tranquilizers and never tried to move or lie down. He kept his cheerful attitude the entire time.

Nina attributes Pasha's ability to handle his lay up to his background. Any other horse would try to move, fight his confinement, and attempt to lie down. Pasha's circus training un-doubtedly saved his life. He had been taught to stand still, and stand still he did.

He put up daily with taking antibiotics, both orally and intravenously. He was wrapped and rewrapped and rubbed with DMSO. Yet he never flinched.

One of the good parts of the lay up was the massages. Weekly massages were given in order to keep his blood circulating and promote healing.

The kids who loved Pasha, who had been learning to ride on him, did their part. They would visit with him, eating their lunches outside his stall. Pasha never lacked for attention or com-panionship.

For seven weeks Pasha remained tied up. The x-rays were encouraging, so after that seven-week period he was finally allowed to be loose in his stall. He could move; he could lie down.

Still nervous about what could happen, Nina took it all very slowly, and was very conservative. After all, this pony had cheated death; she was not about to mess with success!

Yet Pasha had other ideas. He had been loose in his stall for a couple of weeks when one day he opened his door, galloped down the aisle and outdoors to freedom where he raced down the road to his paddock.

Nina's emotions were a curious mixture of panic and ela-tion. Elation, because she couldn't believe how sound Pasha looked. Never did Nina think she would see the pony move again the way he was moving. Panic, because what if this beautiful, sound pony, after enduring so much, got hit by a truck galloping down the road? And what if that galloping had reinjured the leg?

Calling Dr. Durso, Nina cried hysterically into the receiver, "Pasha got out! He galloped down the road."

"Is he lame?" Dr. Durso asked.

Nina's panic slowed a little. "No. Actually he's completely sound."

"I can't get over there for two hours. If he's not lame now, he probably won't be. But we'll know for sure in two hours. If anything is going to show, it will by then."

"And don't," the vet added, "do anything! Don't cold hose, don't wrap, don't give bute. If there's anything wrong, we have to see it."

It was the hardest advice Nina has ever followed in her life. "Don't do anything?" But she had to. She had to make the pony more comfortable, do something for him. Despite that overwhelming desire, she controlled herself. Nina listened to her vet.

When Dr. Durso arrived, Pasha was fine. There was no heat, no swelling, and he remained sound.

Although those surrounding him hadn't realized it was time for Pasha to get on with life, he had. "I'm fine," he was telling Nina. "I'm going out. I'm done with standing in my stall, and if you won't let me out, I will."

Pasha had opened the latch on his stall to escape. He could have done it anytime once he was untied, but he didn't. He waited. When he was ready, he opened it. He knew it was the right time.

Pasha is back to giving lessons. In fact he's back to jumping again, racing around courses with his tail proudly held high in the air. There is no indication that he ever had an injury. Pasha was smart enough to be a good patient when he had to be, and smart enough to know when he no longer needed to be a patient. When others would have put him down, Pasha was lucky enough to be with someone who gave him a chance.

And, true to his unspoken word, he never did any of his tricks during one of Nina's lessons.

HEROES FOR HORSES

⤵ The Day No Horse Went
to Slaughter

One hundred and sixty-three horses were facing ship-
ment to a slaughter plant that May day in Sugarcreek, Ohio. But
there was good news for them. The kill buyers all left with empty
trailers.

Jennifer Swanson and Victoria McCullough had teamed
up to give every one of the horses a second chance. Jennifer,
founder of Pure Thoughts Horse Rescue, rescues horses bound for
slaughter and other abused equines. Victoria is the founder of The
Triumph Project, whose mission is to enlighten the world to the
truth about horse slaughter and to put an end to it.

Many people are under the misconception that horses are
no longer slaughtered in this country. Although American slaugh-
terhouses were closed, tens of thousands of horses are still shipped
(under incredibly cruel conditions) across the border to Mexico
and Canada for slaughter.

Jennifer founded Pure Thoughts about seven years ago. At
the time she was completely immersed in the corporate world. Her
only exposure to horses was as a "horse show mom," supporting
her daughter Camille by paying the bills on her horse and attending her shows.

Life as Jennifer knew it came to an end the day Camille came running home from a yard sale and insisted that they go to the bank right away. Camille needed to empty out her bank account; she'd found something she absolutely had to have.

Jennifer suspected it was the scooter her daughter had always dreamed of. Instead, after going to the bank and taking out all her savings, Camille led her back to the yard sale and showed Jennifer a photo of a small, scrawny horse: a horse that was bound for slaughter. There were four other horses in the photo album that hadn't been adopted; Jennifer adopted them all and arranged for the horses to be shipped to them.

Jennifer had no idea that horses in this country went to slaughter. She was horrified, but glad that Camille had alerted her, and that she had been able to give the five horses a safe home.

It didn't take long after their arrival before people started dropping by to meet the new horses. The visitors would fall in love with the horses and adopt them. That meant there was room for more. Jennifer replaced them with other horses that needed rescue. And so Pure Thoughts was born.

Pure Thoughts made it a habit to rescue horses from the Sugarcreek auction for several reasons. It was a kill auction, and it was one that no other horse rescue attended. There was no one there for the horses, and so Pure Thoughts came.

It was miserable, though, for those from Pure Thoughts who attended the auction. They knew that they only had the resources to save some of the horses. It felt like they were playing God, knowing that the horses they didn't take would face a terrifying death.

Victoria McCullough read about Pure Thoughts in a Phelps Media Group press release. Victoria had horses of her own and had no idea of the brutal end that so many wonderful horses came to. She had been led to believe that horses that go to slaughter were old and lame, and that's what she expected to see when she came to visit Pure Thoughts. Instead, she saw healthy, loving, athletic horses of all ages.

Although Pure Thoughts is very good at rescuing horses, they didn't have anyone who could be a voice for those horses in Washington. Victoria brought that ability to the rescue. While rescues save the horses, Victoria can help bring about the changes for horses that they so desperately need.

One of Victoria's first moves was to arrange for a group of Pure Thought's rescue horses to be part of the opening ceremonies at the National Horse Show. The horses received a standing ovation.

To help bring about changes in laws and attitudes, Victoria needed facts and figures. To come up with those facts, she decided upon a plan. The combined forces of The Triumph Project and Pure Thoughts would rescue all of the horses at Sugarcreek during one auction. But with that auction barely a week away, only a short time was available to arrange all the details of buying, holding, and transporting more than 150 horses.

Despite the short notice, the combined efforts of the two groups pulled it off. As the auction went along, Victoria bid on all the horses. Once the owner of the auction caught on to what was happening, he got angry. He raised the prices. It didn't matter. She kept bidding. This time there was no playing God. All of the horses were leaving with Pure Thoughts.

A holding facility had been located where the horses could be kept until they were able to be shipped to Pure Thoughts in Florida. Unable to obtain Coggins at the auction, the rescue needed to keep the horses elsewhere while awaiting the requisite paperwork for shipping. And then there were the logistics of lining up shipping for 163 horses!

Of all the horses saved that day, contrary to the myths promulgated by pro-slaughter forces, only seven were too old or infirm to have useful lives or any quality of life. Victoria says, "The group was full of lovely serviceable horses including Paints, Thoroughbreds, draft horses, and adorable ponies."

Once the horses made it safely to Florida, Pure Thoughts was overjoyed with the amazing response they received from the community. Jennifer says, "Vets and farriers came out to help, to offer their services. Every day people were calling to help." Mr. Isaac Arrguetty let them use his Mida Farm in Wellington for about 40 of the incoming horses. Joe Norrick, and Stu and Roberta Feinberg also stepped in to house the rescues.
People came out to help, to visit the horses, and to adopt them. Those who had never been to Pure Thoughts were stunned by the quality of these horses that had been thrown away.

In less than four months after their rescue, half of the horses had new homes. Now winning at barrel racing, driving, and jumping, exploring trails with their new families, and enjoying lives as well-loved pets, these horses got the happy ending that all horses deserve.

"I have bought wonderful things for myself during my life," says Victoria, "but providing funds for the rescue of these horses is truly the best purchase I've ever made. If every one of us can open a stall door to a horse in need, there wouldn't be horses at auction facing a painful death. No horse should have an end like that."

"This world is far from perfect," believes Victoria, "but we can all make a difference."

⟿ Saving the Wild Horses

Two thousand mustangs faced death: euthanasia from the Bureau of Land Management. Their crime? They hadn't been adopted and were "too expensive to feed."

The land available for the mustangs to live on had been reduced by an astounding 19 million acres. As a result, the government rounded up more and more horses. Besides the 2,000 on death row, many thousands more are confined in small pens. Born to a life of freedom, these horses are instead jailed.

But the death sentence was commuted. Animal welfare groups, and Madeleine Pickens, wife of billionaire T. Boone Pickens, came to the horses' rescue. A horse owner herself and breeder of Thoroughbreds, including the renowned Cigar, Mrs. Pickens was not about to let these American icons be slaughtered. She came up with a plan to save not just the mustangs on death row, but the entire herd of "unwanted" horses.

Her actions earned her the title of ABC News Person of the Week.

But it wasn't awards Madeleine Pickens was looking for. As an animal lover Madeleine has always considered that people must be responsible for the care of animals. Animals don't have a voice, so we have the responsibility to take care of them.

After Hurricane Katrina blindsided our southern states, Mrs. Pickens stepped in and went to Baton Rouge, Louisiana, where she rescued approximately 800 cats and dogs, transporting them to other states where adoptive homes for them were found.

When she heard that thousands of mustangs were about to be killed, she wouldn't sit still for it. These mustangs, she said, are "our national treasure." The horses date back in time to the Spanish Conquistadors. They roam free on federal land in ten western states, sharing that land with cattle.

Madeleine has formed a plan to create a sanctuary for these horses, where they can roam free as they have for generations and never have to fear being rounded up, imprisoned, or destroyed. No wild horse will be turned away from this sanctuary. Also on the agenda is neutering some of the horses to prevent overpopulation problems. The location and details for this permanent, safe place are currently being worked out.

Besides providing wild horses a safe haven, the sanctuary will be open to visitors, allowing them the opportunity to see our country's living heritage: wild horses. There will be lodges and campsites available for tourists. And the icing on the cake is the $700 to $800 million a year the sanctuary will save for taxpayers.

Who says one person can't make a difference?

To read about sanctuary specifics, updates, or to find out how you can help, check out: www.madeleinepickens.com.

COMPETITORS

⤳ JABBERWOCKY

Anna Vaculik hears the question again and again. "Is that Jabberwocky?" It seems that everyone knows the bright chestnut gelding. He's "been there, done that:" living, and competing, throughout North America.

Beginning life as "My Risky Business," Jabberwocky is a Canadian Thoroughbred who started his working life as a racehorse. He raced three times, winning $900. So ended that career.

He was purchased by a Canadian woman who evented him for a couple of years, doing well enough to place third at the Fair Hills two star event. Soon she and Jabs moved to British Columbia for two years, so that she could be with her boyfriend.

Jabs next surfaces in Georgia, where he had a brief career in the jumper ring. Apparently he proved too hot for his rider, so he was sold to Michelle Guidry: back to the world of eventing.

Michelle was a working student for Olympians Karen and David O'Connor, and Jabs moved to their farm in The Plains, Virginia. Michelle competed and won with Jabs in numerous one star and two star events, as well as the Intermediate Division at Young Rider competitions, scoring a Gold Medal with the horse. They had top finishes in such illustrious events as the Ledyard Farm Three Day Event *, Radnor Hunt International Three day Event ** and both Southern Pines and Pine Hill Horse Trials (in the Open Intermediate Division).

Unfortunately, Jabs sustained a hock injury which prevented him from doing anything beyond the Preliminary Level. After being turned out for a period to recuperate, he was put up for sale. One of the other working students had been an employee of Tracie Ruzicka. Tracie runs an event barn, Rivendell Riding Academy in Clinton Corners, New York. The former employee alerted Tracie that a very talented and well schooled horse was available.

Much of Jabs' life thus far had been spent learning. Now, the tables turned. Jabs became the teacher, training several of Tracie's students to ride. Tracie loves to mount her students "on horses that know more than they do," and she could not have found a better choice than Jabs.

Initially Jabs was a total hothead: becoming so excited in the start box that he would rear. But once the countdown ended and he shot out of the box, he focused completely on the task ahead of him. Tracie says he was always a lovely mover and, having come out of the O'Connor's barn, possessed brilliant training. In addition, he was a very, very safe jumper and had perfect barn manners.

No one in Tracie's barn could fail to notice the striking chestnut, or not notice his astonishing predilection for always being at the top of the pack. Young Jessie Smith was riding at the barn, and she couldn't take her eyes off of Jabs.

Jessie's horse had developed asthma and could no longer compete. When the rider showing Jabs lost her enthusiasm for eventing, Tracie suggested that Jessie give Jabs a try. It was love at first ride. Jessie was turning 12, and she received Jabberwocky for a birthday gift.

Jessie says, "He was so awesome; I felt like a million bucks when I rode him. He's amazing at dressage, and it was just wonderful to have a horse that always knew exactly what he needed to do, and you always knew he would do it." Jessie showed Jabs at Novice and did one Training Level event with him. "He's such a performer, so terrific in dressage, and I never had a rail with him. Jabs is only 15.3—so little, but so mighty."

Jabs continued his winning ways with Jessie, scoring numerous victories, and never placing lower than third. Jabs, says Jessie, "taught me so much. I wouldn't be where I am today if not for him. He loves what he does and wants to be the best. Because of that, he made me want to be the best rider I could be. I always think about how lucky I was to have him: he taught me 'this is how eventing is done.' Anyone who has had him in their life is lucky; he's touched everyone who's been around him. He's a once-in-a-lifetime horse."

Jabs knew how good he was in competition and extracted a price for it in the barn. Jessie says, "He's a prince: if he didn't get his treats right away, he would get annoyed with me and turn away. He loves his Lucky Charms; it seemed amazing that I was 12 years old and I had a horse who loved Lucky Charms."

Jessie's parents called Jabs their insurance policy because they knew he would take care of their daughter. Joe, her dad, was comforted by the knowledge that his daughter was mounted so safely. He says, "When you got Jabs ready for cross-country, you'd get him tacked up, and leave him there for a few minutes. You'd come back and he would be asleep. That's how confident he was in what he was doing." Joe adds that "Jabs would always get the kids in a decent position dressage-wise, and then in jumping it was like he was on auto-pilot. He gave the kids a taste of what it's like to strive to always win, because he had all the tools to do it. With Jabs you weren't just in the top ten: you won. And when Jessie went out hacking on him, it was a comfort to know that she would be coming back safely."

One year Jessie decided to show Jabs in some jumper classes at the Garden State Horse Show. Despite a huge class, Jabs was champion in the division, cutting seconds off the time of his closest competitors. His speed served him well on cross-country courses, too: Jessie never had trouble making the time.

Unfortunately, Jessie grew too tall, too fast, for Jabs. After having him for only two years, she had to sell him.

Tracie had another student waiting in the wings for her favorite teacher. Just like Jessie, Jabs changed Dr. Terry Gotthelf's life. Jabs was Terry's first horse. As a child, Terry had ridden on weekends until she turned 16. Then she quit for 30 years. When she and her husband bought a house in upstate New York, it was Terry's opportunity to take up riding again on weekends. But this time she had hit that slippery slope. The next thing she knew, she had leased a horse. After a year and a half of that, she was ready to buy one. That's when Jabs entered the picture.

Instead of riding on weekends, Terry now rode five days a week, and took up eventing. Phrasing it carefully, Terry doesn't say that she evented Jabs, instead she asserts, "He evented me." He was so good at the dressage phase, says Terry, that "You could get on his back, not know anything, and win at dressage."

At event after event, trainers came up to Terry and told her "That's a really nice horse." At first, Terry didn't fully comprehend just what a special horse she owned. But she got the message.

Cross-country was another story. Jabs' sense of speed had been predetermined by his years as an upper level horse. The speeds for training and novice were simply not part of his vocabulary. As a result, Terry's cross-country experiences consisted of being run away with.

Jabs had always been a wild child in the start box, and one day he gave Terry the ride of her life. He and Terry were at an event at Rhine Valley, while Tracie was coaching students at another event. Because of his antics, Tracie would lead him in to the start box, turn him around, and feed him to keep him quiet until it was time to go. Then Jabs would explode out of the box.

With Tracie's absence, the experience unfolded quite differently. Jabs and Terry went into the start box, and they came out of the start box. The only difference was in the direction they came out. They had not turned around to face the entrance. After they entered the box, Jabs plunged ahead and jumped right out the back. The fence composing the start box was at least four and a half feet high.

The episode is still talked about in eventing circles in the Hudson Valley. And yes, Terry did manage to stay on.

In the three years she had Jabs, Terry says, "He taught me everything."

When Tracie ran out of suitable students for Jabs to teach, she approached another trainer, Lisa Winkler, at a show. She knew that one of Lisa's students was struggling to event with an inappropriate mount. "I have the perfect horse for you," she told Lisa. And she did.

Anna had been riding a former show jumper who wanted nothing to do with the sport of eventing, and never missed an opportunity to make that known to her.

Jabs was moved to Lisa's barn, Valley Crest Farm in Millbrook New York, and Anna began riding him. At first she was rather unsure of him, and didn't know what to expect. It didn't take long for uncertainty to turn to love. "All my cross-country fears disappeared with him. My goals went from not getting eliminated to getting good dressage scores and double-clear jumping rounds."

Jabs had been out of work for nine months when he came to Lisa's barn. Anna had to learn how to care for an older horse, and how to condition him after a long period of inactivity. Anna declares, "He's taught me so much, not just about riding but about horse care."

At their first event together, Eastern New York Dressage and Combined Training Association, Jabs "made it a lot of fun. I was nervous about the water because the other horse would just stop. Jabs just trotted right through it, and I had the time of my life. He made the day perfect."

The "one summer" that Jabs was supposed to spend with

Anna has now become two years. They have competed (and won) at numerous events including the United States Pony Club Championships in Lexington, Virginia, and qualified for the American Eventing Championships in Illinois (but didn't attend). Anna used to approach an event with trepidation. Now, "I go in thinking it's going to be fun. I don't have to worry about anything any more. I trust him. He's changed the way I ride, and helped me understand what it means to be an eventer."

In their first event in 2009, at King Oak Farm in Massachusetts, Anna and Jabs won the Junior Horsemanship Award presented by the *Massachusetts Horse* magazine. The award was voted on by the judges and stewards and is given to "the exhibitor exemplifying all that is good in our young riders today."

Anna's mom Beth says, "I look at him as a gift. I've watched him give my daughter confidence, teach her to win, to work hard, and that he'll always be there and always bring you back. He's been pivotal in Anna's life."

"He's part of our family. We love him."

Jabberwocky had the experience of competing, and winning, at the top levels of the sport. Once he could no longer compete at that level he took up the job of coach, teaching riders what eventing is all about, and letting them experience the thrill of victory. Still competing in his mid-20's, Jabs has influenced scores of lives and changed everyone he's been involved with for the better.

Next time you spot a small chestnut gelding with a big blaze doing remarkable dressage, or putting in an awesome cross-country round, go introduce yourself. You may have just met Jabberwocky.

⤳ Silver Aside
by Anne Moss

Often, I am asked why I am showing aside, when dressage astride is challenging enough, even for Olympians. It all boils down to the mountain climber wisdom of "because it is there" and if I don't, who will? This is the challenge part...you are supposed to jump up, screaming, "I will! I will!"

Joan Bennett paved my way by being the first person to earn a United States Dressage Federation (USDF) Bronze Medal by getting two scores of 60% at first, second and third levels. I must admit, getting a 60% is pretty easy at first and second levels, but that is where, easy ends. I guess the requirements of counter canter, the canter half pass and lead changes raise the bar considerably and that pesky collection issue....We scored many a 58%, 59.73%, and 59.8%...and every time we missed a 60%, I knew the Bronze would taste even sweeter when I eventually made it. Which we did, all in one season, in 2001!

It was incredible to join Joan in the USDF Bronze Club. Shelly Liggett and ISSO (International Side Saddle Association) kindly presented me with a tin tiara celebrating my accomplishment. I actually wore it over my riding helmet to a dressage lesson once, but have since stopped for fear I may wear it out. After all, it is the only one I have.

Now what? You might think it was on to the Silver Medal! Sounds like a reasonable climb right up the ladder. The problem is that I am not really a dressage queen, even wearing the tiara; you can tell I am a phony. The Silver Medal requires two scores of 60% at fourth level and Prix St. George (PSG). By the way, Helium is a common off-the-track Thoroughbred, and acts like it, which makes dressage only reasonable if followed by cross country and show jumping, right? He has been incredibly tolerant of my dressage fantasy, as long as, he gets to hunt once or twice a month, September through March, to regain his sanity.

Many dressage lessons later, a lot of circles in the pasture later, we have figured out a little about collection, lead changes, half-pass and pirouettes. All this being very tricky for a horse that prefers not to bend or go sideways, thank you. He squeaks and squeals excessively whenever he has an opinion, which is every time you use your leg. Incredible support and generosity from a neighbor and a dressage buddy has kept me at it, year-round practicing indoors twice a week. Support and "rooting-on" from the U.S. side-saddle community has bolstered my thin confidence and made it seem important that I try for the "Silver."

Joan Bennet earned 60% scores at fourth level aside, but never made the Prix St. George scores. My friend Sarah Duclos got a 60% at PSG in 2002, on her lovely Arab Lenny, that was encouraging.

While experimenting the past few years showing aside, I have revamped my warm-up routine to accommodate the increased difficulty at Fourth Level and Prix St. George. I had always done the whole warm-up aside through Third Level, but found it easier to gain the suppleness and balance I need to be competitive at the higher levels when astride. The formula that seems to work best so far is: hand walk and graze for 15 minutes then spend 10-15 minutes on the lunge line in a halter in the trot to get him moving really freely, then tack up astride for 20 minutes, where I work primarily on getting him moving forward in front of my two legs, working some of the movements of the test comfortably. Untack, get dressed, tack-up aside with the KN [Karl Niedersuss side saddle] and finish with 10-15 minutes warm-up aside.

Our first outing in 2003 was at Morven Park in Leesburg, VA at the VADA/NOVA Spring Show in April. Helium likes Morven Park, which makes a difference when riding a fickle creature. He makes it quite clear regarding his preferences in footing, stabling and atmosphere, so I try to show where he is happy. There, we had the opportunity to ride the Fourth Level test two, for Sandra Hotz.

Fourth–2, includes trot and canter half pass, collected, medium and extended in all gaits, quarter pirouettes in canter, half pirouettes in walk, 8 meter trot circles, single flying changes, and a line of three changes every fourth stride, yikes! The test scored; mostly 6's in the trot work and 7's in the canter, with a few 5's and one 4 on the line of changes, with all 6's for collective marks. An impressive effort so early in the season, that scored a 60.698% and secured our first qualifying score towards the Silver Medal!

Our efforts at PSG that weekend earned 56% and 58%, which was encouraging, but not making the mark.

Many shows later, having earned 55, 58, 58% scores at Fourth Level, we had our last show at the NJ Horse Park in October. No pressure! But we were pretty tired of coming so close…

Sunday 10/05/03, NJ Horse Park -I had an 8:30AM ride time, day three of getting up with the birds and showing! The test was in the outdoor arena, Jan Gille judged the 4-1 test again and I had great hopes of bettering the 59% of the day before. Lunge, school astride and finish the warm-up aside seems to be the trick. He felt much more forward, though a bit lower in his frame, which is a trade off and seemed only fair as it was the third day in a row I had asked this dear creature to show aside. He went better than ever, though kicked out in one lead change and I forgot the last two short diagonals and changes, error minus two points.

I felt more in control of my balance and kept a steadier feel of his mouth. Much to my delight, we were rewarded with a 62.09%, the prize I was after, one step closer to a Silver Medal. My mom and my sister Amy were there to help and cheerlead; it was wonderful to have them there to share it with me. It was lovely to end the season with the Fourth Level scores under our belt, two scores of 58% at PSG just nipping at the heels of the coveted 60%.

Over the Winter 2003-2004, we fox hunted half a dozen times, tried to buckle down and school the harder movements at PSG by riding a lot indoors. We also participated in a four-day clinic with Charles deKunffy and two clinics with George Williams.

The PSG includes collected, medium and extended gaits, shoulders-in (in the trot), trot half pass, canter half pass, zigzag with flying changes, walk and canter half pirouettes, halt and rein back, counter canter, lines of changes every fourth and every third stride. Yikes!

Back at Morven Park for their Spring show in April 2004, we rode the PSG test for Judge Margaret Freeman and scored 62.25%, we placed fourth out of fourteen rides, which was a great bonus. Half of the scores on this test were 7's, some 6's and an 8 on a walk half-pirouette! We had lower scores on the tempi changes and canter pirouettes, which are the hardest movements, with collective marks of 7, 6, 6, and 7. He warmed up a bit on the wild side but proceeded to go beautifully in the arena with the most forward and consistent PSG test to date. It was a real thrill to have our winter homework pay off, in spades.

Now I was excited, really excited about the prospect of the Silver Medal becoming a reality. Our training was definitely pumped up through the rest of April, in preparation for the May show at Morven Park, where we hoped for a repeat performance. We rode aside in a clinic with George Williams the weekend before, which greatly helped me improve Helium's attentiveness to my aids and balance in the turns and lateral work.

My hopes were dangerously high now and I may have become obsessed with Silver Medal tunnel vision. I was wholly distracted and fairly unfit to live with. My weekend horse show buddy, Deb Tsang, tried valiantly to temper my expectations with well-reasoned reality checks, but to no avail...Saturday, May 8, 2004,we rode the PSG for Judge Ida Anderson and had a consistent go with the exception of one communication error on an 8-meter circle that resulted in a score of 1, (Auuurg). Otherwise, the test scored mostly 6's, with some 7's, a 5 on one canter pirouette and a 4 on the changes every three strides, rider lost count! We were rewarded by being fourth in a 15 horse field and earned a 60% even!

After seeing the score posted at the secretary's stand, I did a jig and chanted 'I got my silver medal!'

For hours following, I celebrated with friends and stable neighbors with a bottle of bubbly and chocolate chip cookies. Of course, Helium had free choice of carrots, apples and his favorite medley of horse treats.

I had been preparing his digestive system for this moment by spoiling him rotten with treats for the past eight years. It may have been a bit ambiguous to him to discern the weight of his achievement by goodie volume.

The following day we rode the PSG again aside for Judge William Solyntjes and had an even better ride, scoring a 60.5%, which was confirmation of Helium's ability at this level.

The journey I have taken with Helium, riding at this level is a dream come true, aside or astride. The generosity and willingness on Helium's part, which has enabled our progress, has been a true gift. He has gone above and beyond the equine call of duty. He has tolerantly waded with me through mistakes and confusion, again and again. Somehow he figured out what to do with the convoluted aside aids, I ply upon him, true equine genius. I have learned so much and have been supported by so many wonderful people while pursuing this sideways dressage experiment that turned into an exciting and enriching chapter of my life.

My family and friends will attest that I am floating in the clouds. "SILVER" clouds, that is.

⤳ TWIN POND DISCO KID

One could say that the story of Twin Pond Disco Kid is a rags to riches story. However, we're not talking money here. Instead, as owner Karen Myers said, "it's about trust, love, and companionship."

In 1991 Karen was looking for a barn with an indoor in which to board her Quarter Horse All For Remo for the winter. When she contacted Sonja Wood of Sonja Wood Stables in Afton, New York, she discovered Sonja had one stall available. Her mare moved in.

That was when Karen first became acquainted with Twin Pond Disco Kid, a Morgan stallion. Better known as Bucky for his habit as a youngster of running across his field bucking incessantly, at that point the stallion was 10 years old and "a shell of a horse." He betrayed no emotion, no heart. His behavior was angry and distrustful, lunging at the front of his stall with bared teeth, warding off any who might approach.

Yet, Karen could see a spark in his eyes. She was intrigued, wondering what lay behind his mask of fear and obvious distrust of people. Inquiring of Sonja, she learned that the horse had been physically abused by an earlier trainer.

A short time later, Sonja asked Karen if she might be interested in showing Bucky in Western Pleasure for his owner Jackie Honeck. Karen didn't hesitate for a second: she would love to!

As she began working with the handsome stallion, his true self began to emerge. The light Karen had spied in his eye had betrayed who Bucky really was, and the two began to develop a bond.

Throughout the spring and summer, the two worked hard. Although they were doing well, Karen could feel that the horse was capable of so much more. His balance and athleticism could serve him well in many different disciplines. And Bucky had become bored with railwork. He needed something more challenging to keep him interested.

Sadly, the time that Karen had been hired to show Bucky was drawing to an end.

Karen didn't know how she would be able to come to the barn and not ride Bucky anymore. At the New York Regional Show, she talked to Sonja about how hard it was going to be to end the relationship that she and the stallion had developed.

"Buy him." Sonya advised.

Although Jackie had no plans to sell him, selling him to Karen was an entirely different story. Jackie could see the bond that was developing between Karen and Bucky. She drew up terms for the sale, making it very easy for Karen to purchase him. Karen took Sonja's advice and remains ever grateful for Jackie's generosity.

Bucky was now Karen's horse, and her first ever Morgan horse.

That fall Karen met local reining horse trainer Ed Cridge. Impressed with how Ed handled and trained his horses, Karen contacted him a week later and asked if he would help her "make this horse be the best he could be."

Once a week Karen and Bucky went to Ed's farm for a lesson. These were some of the best lessons of Karen's life. The remainder of the week she would work on their assignment, and spend countless hours with Bucky developing trust and respect with him.

Karen will never forget the first time she knelt in Bucky's stall. The horse hit the back wall and started climbing it. Her heart aching for the stallion, she vowed that he would not spend the rest of his life living in fear.

Ed told her, "A great horse cannot be ruined, and if they ever find their person to connect with, they will become what they always were meant to be." He taught Karen a great deal about bringing a horse to its full potential one step at a time.

Karen says, "Patience was the key to unlocking this horse's great soul." Once that bond of trust developed, "There was nothing that he wouldn't do for me."

As Bucky emerged from his shell, he thrived on the new training program. Spanning three years, Ed's system replaced Bucky's old ways of going and reasoning with a whole new set of commands, cues, exercises, relaxation, and trust.

At times when Ed and Karen thought they had hit Bucky's mental or physical limit they would modify something and Bucky would rise to the next level. He taught Karen how to look at what she was doing as his trainer and to evaluate and change her techniques to get the desired results out of him. In addition, they discovered that Bucky was a natural at reining, and took to the sport with interest and enthusiasm.

By the next spring, Bucky had developed more self-confidence, and his willing to please persona began to blossom. The more he won, the more he liked to win. Initially, Karen showed him in seven different disciplines, and he was a force to be reckoned with in all of them.

Showing in the Morgan arena from 1992-1995, Karen and Bucky won countless titles and year-end awards. She'd also begun to show him a little in reining, and they won the Grand National Non-Pro Reining Title in 1992, 1993, and 1995. In 1995 Karen showed him in Morgan shows in Classic Riding and Driving, Hunter, Western Pleasure, and Over Fences classes, as well as at National Reining Horse Association shows. At the Ohio State Fair NRHA Show, out of 113 Limited Non-Pro entries, Bucky and Karen finished 13th. They headed to the Grand National, and Karen's sights were further set on winning the Non-Pro World

Champion Reining Title.

She and Bucky took the Grand National Reining Title, which qualified them for the World show. This was the first time the show had offered the Non-Pro World Champion Reining Title.

Unfortunately, Bucky managed to get hurt in his stall. Karen spent countless hours hosing his leg, and got him sound enough to compete for the Non-Pro title. She received the attending vet's approval to do so. Despite that, Karen remained concerned about her horse. So concerned, in fact, that she lost her focus while showing: throwing in an extra spin and receiving a zero for their score.

Lesson learned. Karen wanted more than anything to win a world title on Twin Pond Disco Kid. Yet she was splitting her energy, showing in several divisions and at both Morgan and NRHA competitions. Ed counseled her, advising that if she wanted to win a world title then she needed to concentrate on nothing but that.

To get Bucky ready to win the Worlds, Ed told her it was her job to manage his career and put him in the best possible situations to accomplish that goal. Karen took the excellent advice, and, in 1996, she and Bucky competed only at NRHA shows. She took him in the Grand National Non-Pro qualifier as a warm-up so that when she and Twin Pond Disco Kid walked into the arena as the last draw of the 1996 World Champion Non-Pro Reining class, he was ready to take on the world.

He did. All the hours of hard work, the ups and downs of showing, the injuries to be cared for and overcome, had paid off. Karen and Bucky had won their World title. Karen was immeasurably proud of her horse. Bucky had come countless miles; transforming from an aloof shell to a partner that would give his all to his best friend.

When they returned home, everyone celebrated with a party at the local fire hall. Bucky was the guest of honor and couldn't get enough attention.

Ed once again gave Karen great advice: "Stay out of his way and let him show the world what he knows, and always, always trust him."

For the next three years, Bucky and Karen stuck to the NRHA shows. Judge after judge approached Karen to find out what Bucky's breeding might be. When she told them he was a Morgan, they would just smile and tell her what a nice, nice horse he was.

With his tremendous competitive success, Bucky began to develop his own fan club in the reining world. Many die-hard Quarter Horse lovers had their eyes opened to the possibilities of a Morgan who possessed the same athletic abilities as his cousins, but stamped his performances with his added bit of style. While his spins were similar, his frame during his circles was more collected, making his circle profile absolutely stunning. His gorgeous head, softly flexed at the chin and poll, clean throatlatch, rounded neck, rounded knee, and collected round rump could not fail to pile on the points.

Bucky could stop a mile with his shoulders, just snapping his knees up as he walked along in the front, and he could literally run backwards.

Their talent and style earned invitations for Bucky and Karen to perform at such diverse venues as Equine Affaire's Phantasia, The New York State Fair, The Syracuse International Horse Show, The New England and New York Regionals, and the American Morgan Horse Association's Celebration of the Breed.

From the anti-social stallion Karen first met, Bucky went on to become the horse that she put novice riders on for a trail ride, and the one she chose to pony his foals off of. Bucky went out with his mares and foals, and Karen would often look out and see him and his foals off grazing by themselves.

Bucky's influence extended to many areas of Karen's life. She established Myers Performance Morgans based around him.

She became a Certified Equine Sports Massage Therapist so that Bucky could have his own masseuse. Because of the reining industry's open acceptance of her Morgan reining horses, she became an NRHA judge. Most important to Karen have been the many wonderful people she has met because of the foals Bucky helped produce.

In 2006 she showed Bucky's daughter Wintermoon Waltz With Me, owned by her niece Stefanie Kuppinger, to the Non-Pro Reining World title despite showing her only once before going to the world show. The mare possessed all of Bucky's heart and desire to please. It was just like showing Bucky: simply trust her and she would trust you.

One of Bucky's great legacies is that he is a great founding sire of top Morgan reining horses. He has blessed many of his foals with his great heart, conformational strength, quiet mind, above average intelligence, and most of all, his willingness to please people.

One of Karen's fondest memories was of when she and Bucky were invited to perform at the New England Regional 2007 Grand Ole Champions evening. To have Twin Pond Disco Kid included among some of the greatest Morgans representing his era was the ultimate in honors. Karen hadn't ridden him in public in at least five years, and all the memories came flooding back to her when she swung her leg over him and rode through the crowd. The number of people that stopped her to talk about their memories of seeing him show was amazing. It was such a humbling experience to look out and see all his Morgan fans cheering for him as he walked into the ring one last time.

Bucky knew why he was there and he went all out to put on a show for his fans. Although Karen had no intention of performing sliding stops with him, Bucky had his own ideas. He had a crowd to please, and he was not about to let them down.

That was the last time Karen ever rode him. When she hopped off him and hugged him, her eyes filled with tears. She thanked him for all the great memories he had given her, for all her dreams that he had helped her fulfill, and for the great team they had become. It was a perfect ending for his career.

Twin Pond Disco Kid gave Karen his heart, and touched hers forever.

⤳ COUNT ON ME

Danielle Buchheit first met him when he was only three weeks old. Even then, he was a knockout. A bright chestnut with four white socks that seemed to extend right up to his body, the Thoroughbred colt exuded quality.

"Couldn't you have put in an order for more chrome?" Danielle teased the colt's breeder, Jenny Fisher.

Jenny was Danielle's trainer, and along with Danielle's grey Thoroughbred Heartlight they formed a nearly unbeatable team. Heartlight (a.k.a Harley) had had a fabulously successful career as a show horse in the working hunters and now he and Danielle were racking up championships on every level in the sidesaddle division.

Sadly, due to Jenny's hectic schedule, she and Danielle had to go their separate ways. Jenny spent so much time on the road that it had become very difficult for Danielle to find time when she was home to work with her. Danielle searched for a new trainer, and soon began working with Kit Roszko of Jackson, New Jersey. After that, she didn't see much of Jenny.

Danielle began her riding career early, and it would have been even earlier had her Dad, Leon Buchheit, had his way. He had Danielle when he was 36, and it was always his fondest dream that his daughter should ride. One day he packed her up in the car and took her with him to Glenmere, a riding school near their home. He found an instructor and told her that he wanted his daughter to have riding lessons.

"Where is your daughter?" the instructor asked.

"In the car," her Dad replied.

The instructor walked to the car. Inside was a car seat containing an infant only a few months old, unable even to sit up on her own yet.

"You might want to bring her back when she's a little older," the instructor advised.

Three years after they'd lost touch, Danielle got a phone call from Jenny.

"Do you remember that gorgeous colt?" Jenny asked. "He's for sale and he would make a fantastic hunter or side-saddle horse."

"Remember him?" thought Danielle. "Of course!" She could never forget such a beautiful horse. Danielle told Jenny that Kit, who was scheduled to come up that week, would take a look at him.

The stunning colt couldn't fail to impress Kit. She let several of her clients know about him. But everyone passed him by. At 16 hands, they felt that he was too small.

As for Danielle, much as she loved the horse, she had Heartlight. She didn't need another horse.

Jenny worked hard on Danielle, sure that this would be a great horse for her. "He'd be a terrific sidesaddle horse" she told her.

"I don't need another horse," was Danielle's reply.

But there is one constant throughout all of our lives: change. In time, Heartlight developed melanomas. He no longer wanted to jump, and had to be retired.

Hearing about it, Jenny seized her opportunity. Nothing would shake her belief that this horse was born to be with Danielle. Jenny called her. "I hear you're looking for a horse."

"Yes, I do need a horse," Danielle told her. "But you don't

understand. I'm not in the same league as your clients. I can't afford him."

Jenny persisted. She tried a new tactic. "He's going to have to spend the winter out with the broodmares." Maybe Danielle would succumb to guilt.

Danielle held firm. "I don't spend money I don't have."

"I'll give you time payments," Jenny tempted.

Danielle repeated "No. If I don't have the money I don't spend it."

The horse spent the winter with the broodmares.

In March, Jenny resumed her battle. "I'll give you my rock bottom price and I'll let you take him on trial."

Danielle fortified her defenses. "I don't want a green horse. I want one that's been there, done that. I'm too old for a green horse."

"You'll love him. He's so safe and sane."

In the end, Jenny's tactics prevailed. She was right. Besides being gorgeous and talented, the horse was dependable. Danielle took him on trial, and he turned out to be very easy, with a great mind.

The flashy chestnut was sired by Viscount, a top show horse. Although Jenny had done a fabulous job of starting him, he had not yet been exposed to a sidesaddle. The first time Danielle tried the sidesaddle on him, she was a little anxious. She started by lunging him with it on and he seemed fine, so she decided to give it a go.

She brought him to the mounting block and went to get on. When she put her foot in the stirrup, she didn't realize that her stirrup was only "hooked" through one layer of the stirrup leather. (The sidesaddle stirrup leather has a hook that actually fits through the punched hole in the leather rather then a buckle.) As the hook was only through the outer layer of the leather, when Danielle put her weight in the iron, the leather ripped and she fell to the ground.

The horse just took one step away from the mounting block and looked at her as to say, "What happened?" He never spooked, merely stepped away. Danielle fixed the stirrup, tried to mount again and got on this time. He was fine at the walk, so they trotted and he was fine, so then they cantered and he was fine. It was at that moment Danielle knew she would buy him and that she would name him "Count On Me."

Danielle worked with Count with Kit, and with Annette Mohr. He was purchased in 2003, and he proved so solid and dependable that despite their short time together, they were champions in their division at both Harrisburg and the Metropolitan National that year.

At one point, Danielle called Jenny to make arrangements to pay for Count. When she arrived, out of curiosity she asked what Jenny had named him.

"Count on Me," Jenny told an astonished Danielle.

Danielle got yet another surprise when she received Count's papers. She had lost her Dad, with whom she had maintained a very close relationship, in 1992. He had been her biggest supporter, always encouraging her to ride.

Count was born on June 12, her Dad's birthday.

Danielle and Count on Me have gone on to win at Devon and Washington, as well as additional wins at the biggest shows in the country. In 2008, despite very limited showing Count was Champion again at Harrisburg, and Champion at Side Saddle at the USET and the Zone II Finals.

In addition, the Breyer Company™ came out with a limited edition sidesaddle gift set. Count on Me's image is on the box, so, as Danielle says, "He has his own little Wheatie's box."

Count on Me left an indelible impression on Danielle from their first meeting when he was a tiny baby. It took several years in the making, but he and Danielle were supposed to be together. Some things are just meant to be.

⟶ WHISPER

By Barbara Thomas

The black Morab filly was tiny, just a "whisper of a thing," the barn manager said. She was recently weaned, only six months old, yet it took her just seconds to steal the heart of a 15 year old girl.

"Whisper," as she came to be called, was owned by Dr. Alatis and his family, of Vienna, Virginia. She was the offspring of a Morgan stallion, Little David, and an Arabian mare. The mare lived in an adjoining field to Little David. Not content with her separate paddock, she jumped the fence to join David in his, thus arranging a secret tryst.

Barbara Thomas worked on the farm where Whisper lived, cleaning stalls. On the side, Barbara flipped burgers, and in time she was able to save the $275 to buy the filly she had fallen in love with.

Whisper happily lived outside, sharing a 20 acre pasture with a dozen other horses. However, when she became ill with a respiratory infection it was necessary to bring her inside. No stalls were available, hence temporary measures were taken. The end of the barn aisle was boarded off, a gate was installed, and a baby stall was born.

Whisper proved a great patient, but only while she was sick. Once she was better, she was quick to let everyone know. She backed into the corner of her stall and then leapt out over the front wall.

That was the last time Whisper tolerated a stall. From then on she let her human companions know that she was done with confinement.

Whisper was a teenage girl's dream come true. She and Barbara became constant companions and Barbara loved living out the romance of owning a horse: "My Friend Flicka" come to life. After school, she led Whisper everywhere—to the local store, on the trails, to the swimming hole, and back to her suburban tract house about two miles from the barn. There wasn't a place Barbara went that Whisper didn't follow willingly. Often she just tossed the lead rope over her neck and away they went. Whisper would stop only to eat grass (a Morab trait, Barbara says, "Never starve yourself!"

Soon the black filly with the white blaze began turning grey: every shade of grey...blue roan, steel gray, dappled gray with a black mane and tail, and in the end flea bitten with a dazzling pearl white mane and tail. Gray horses. Barbara says she doesn't know what it is about young girls and gray horses but she thinks it's the dream of a beautiful gray flying over jumps and galloping across the field that puts stars in a girl's eyes.

Poor Whisper was forced to suffer "every idea of proper care that a 15 year old could inflict." Legs were wrapped, bell boots applied; blankets, sheets, baths, braiding, mane pulling, primping, and spraying were all patiently tolerated. Whisper was shown "in-hand" in grooming and color classes at local shows as a yearling. As everyone was showing in pony hunters at the time, that soon became Whisper's career.

In certain places the hunter circuit in the 1970's seemed to follow many Thoroughbred track traditions for training. Horses were "backed" at 18 months, ridden at two and started showing under saddle soon thereafter. Whisper was no exception. She proved herself intelligent and willing to learn. When Barbara bitted and saddled her, she said, "Okay" When she backed her, she stood and said, "Okay" In fact, she wouldn't move at all! Throughout her training, Whisper never said "No."

As a two year old, with just two weeks of riding, she won her first pony hunter under saddle class. Barbara admits she was "quite the little pony hunter snob." With her Crosby Prix de Nations jumping saddle, rolled English bridle, Pytchley riding coat, tall boots and proper pads she made sure to fit the picture. She purchased all except the coat out of her after school earnings. The coat was a gift from her mom, who was terrified of horses and puzzled by her horse-crazy daughter.

Although Whisper tolerated all this for Barbara's sake, deep down Barbara could tell that this was not what the pony wanted out of life.

Fortunately for Whisper her lack of size (13.3) changed her career path. Barbara was nearly 18, just about to age out of showing ponies. She could have given up Whisper or given up the hunter/jumper show world. There was no question about her decision: Whisper wasn't going anywhere!

Barbara learned about something that sounded interesting, Competitive Trail Riding, from her friend Heather Horn. The two went to the very first Old Dominion Endurance ride in Leesburg, Virginia, to help out. No one warned them that one dose of the event would lead to a life long addiction! Whisper and Barbara began trail riding and when Whisper was almost four, she was Grand Champion at the Doncaster 20 mile judged pleasure ride. At four, she completed the Doncaster 40 mile Competitive Trail Ride.

On both rides, Whisper turned into a wild child! Cleverly, though, she behaved in front of the judges. But once out of their sight, all bets were off, she wanted to go! None of this five or seven mile per hour pace, she made it clear that endurance was her sport of choice!

Whisper's career was put on hold while Barbara went to college and then started her "real job" with a medical research firm in Virginia. As Whisper held firm to her goal of never starving herself, she became grossly overweight and out of condition. When Barbara was able to get back in the saddle, she attended every available seminar on endurance and conditioning, worked on rides and slowly brought her mare back into shape.

In 1980 they did their first 50 mile endurance ride at Old Dominion and finished strongly in 11th place. Whisper was a firecracker, pulling Barbara as hard at the end as she did when they started.

It was at this ride that Barbara and Whisper discovered another "gear" at the trot. Never before had Whisper displayed this gait, but her Morgan blood kicked in and suddenly she was doing an incredible "roadster" trot! Her tiny feet barely touched the ground and she pushed off her hindquarters with awesome strength.

Barbara described it as "like riding a sonnet: perfect cadence, perfect balance, airy and smooth!" They passed seasoned horses whose riders' jaws dropped as the little Morab flew by at a trot to their canter. One man looked at her and said that what she was doing was impossible: the length of stride was too big for her small size. Barbara just smiled and waved.

Now that they had some 50 mile rides under their belt, Barbara felt they were ready to try a hundred mile: The Old Dominion 100 to be exact. The ride was to be held in Front Royal, Virginia. It was a tough one, Barbara was warned, and she would need to carefully prepare for it.

Barbara considers herself "Miss Independent" so she decided to ride it "Cavalry"—in other words without a crew. She was also "young and foolish and blessed with an iron butt" so she rode in her Crosby Prix de Nations—in jeans.

The ride was breathtakingly beautiful with "mist rising from the fields as we trotted along the dirt lanes in the silent coolness of the morning." Crossing the Shenandoah at McCoy's Ford was a delight. Endless hay fields led up to the crossing, and continued on the other side, where the backdrop was the majestic Blue Ridge Mountains. The crossing was wide, nearly 300 yards across, and the water was bathtub warm and up to Whisper's shoulder.

Barbara was stocked with baggies of grain and tubes of electrolytes for Whisper; Gatorade, trail mix, and a sandwich for herself. For the first 60 miles, things went well. Then, for the first time in her life, Whisper said, "Whoa, what's going on here? I don't think I like this anymore!" She had, mentally, "hit the wall."

Catching up with another rider, Rick Hill, on his white Arab Amyr Fatez, perked Whisper up and they rode together the rest of the way. Rick was a local resident familiar with the trails. This proved a good thing because Barbara was "never so grateful to have a big white Arab butt" in front of her as she was that night in the pitch dark over Sherman's Gap! Not only did Rick lead the way, he also encouraged Barbara at each vet check not to pull out of the ride.

As they crossed McCoy's in the moonlight, Whisper recognized her surroundings and picked up her pace towards home and food. Coming to a wide creek, Barbara climbed off to cool Whisper in the water, planning to tail up the next climb. But when she hopped back on she discovered that getting wet was a big mistake. She couldn't get off again, her legs were numb. Whisper carried her dead weight up that mountain like a trooper. By the time they finished, Barbara's legs hurt so badly she could hardly move. Her hands were shaking and numb. She went into the tent to get her wet jeans off. Forty-five minutes later, she was still stuck in them.

Matthew Mackay-Smith came to her tent and told her she only had 15 minutes left to present Whisper for final vetting. Seeing her plight, he offered to trot the horse out for her. She looked at him tearfully and said, "You can't, I'm riding Cavalry!"

He was very sweet as he explained to her that she was not in contention as other riders had claimed the top ten, so could he please help her and trot Whisper out. They walked over arm in arm in the early dawn and she watched as her little Morab with the big heart trotted soundly and passed the final vetting.

For a few more years Whisper and Barbara continued to do endurance rides, finishing every ride they started. Then Whisper took a break from competition to have a baby, a filly named Jazz at Dawn.

Whisper then began teaching kids to ride, including a young girl who was blind. Krissy contracted eye cancer at age three and within a year, lost both eyes to the disease. She would come out with her friend Cathy and "see" Whisper with her hands. Whisper sensed that Krissy was a special child and never did anything to frighten her. In one lesson, Cathy was leading Whisper and looking ahead when Whisper slowed and then stopped. Cathy looked back and discovered that Krissy had slipped sideways in the saddle and was halfway to the ground. Whisper knew her little friend was in trouble, so she stopped and patiently waited for help.

Whisper has accompanied Barbara through all the good and bad times of her life. She moved with her to various locations on the east coast and then finally, out to California. Though feisty and opinionated, she's always given 150 %.

At age 27, she foundered. Barbara feared it was the end for her friend. But she fought back bravely and competed in a five mile retired partner's honor ride. She was back in her element and took off with Barbara for the entire five miles!

Twenty-nine now, Whisper has begun to slow down. She and Barbara still hit the trails for short rides. Barbara knows that goodbye isn't that far away. But when it comes, she will fly back to Virginia with Whisper's ashes, and they will climb Sherman's Gap once more. There, Whisper will find her final resting place, where she can welcome every horse from the Old Dominion at the top of their climb.

Only once in a lifetime is someone lucky enough to have a perfect relationship. Barbara found hers at the age of 15 with a tiny black Morab filly named Whisper.

⤳ Bail Me Out (Striker)

By Nikole Ruddy

Striker was born on my grandparent's small farm in Windsor, Connecticut on May 26, 1983. My grandparents, William and Marie Garthwaite, had not expected him to be born yet, so they'd left the farm for a day's outing.

The only person who stayed behind was my aunt, Chris Garthwaite. She was planning to have a relaxing day by the pool. Instead, as soon as my grandparents pulled out of the driveway, their mare, Holly, went into labor. A short time later, Striker was born with a very unrelaxed Aunt Chris by his side!

Striker is a fifth generation descendant from a Thoroughbred/Suffolk cross mare named Lady of Windsor that my grandfather showed in the old Madison Square Garden in 1947. He was conceived as a twin, although we didn't know it at the time. The other twin was stillborn. Striker was a tiny foal. After some initial breaking, he was put out to pasture because he was too small, and the family was busy with other horses in the barn.

Then fate intervened. When I was 12, my aged equitation horse, Striker's uncle Liberty, injured himself and had to be retired. I didn't have another horse to ride. So I pulled Striker out of the pasture and started playing with him. From the start we were buddies. He had a great attitude and was so willing to please that I instantly formed a bond with him. I never worried about him hurting me even though he was very green. Every day after school, I would run down to the pasture, open the gate and let all the horses run up the long hill to the barn. I would jump on Striker bareback and gallop him up the hill with the rest of the horses. He'd let out a buck coming up the hill but it was all in good spirit. I knew when he got to the top of the hill he'd stop and I could hop off and let all the horses into the barn.

I started training Striker with the help of my grandfather, and my aunt, Pat Garthwaite Towle. I took my time, entering him in baby green hunters and moving up slowly to the lower level equitation and hunter classes at local shows. Along with training him for the show ring, I taught him tricks. He would bow on command. My favorite trick was teaching him how to raise his lip as though he had just smelled something bad. If I didn't place well in an equitation class I would ask Striker, "how much does the judge stink?" He would raise his top lip up and everyone around would laugh.

After a couple of years training in the hunter ring, I entered Striker in a 3'6" jumper division at The Pines, in Glastonbury, Connecticut. We had a blast cutting corners and clearing the jumps. He placed first in all three classes that day. I quickly realized that Striker's true calling was in the jumper ring.

In the years to come, my aunt Pat, and Pavel Blaho, partners at Tatra Farm in Clinton Corners, New York, helped me fine tune his jumping ability. Pavel would never call Striker by his name. Instead, he would refer to him as "the little horse." The little horse became a top competitor in the Marshall and Sterling Children and Adult Jumpers. Over the span of 12 years he qualified for the Marshall and Sterling Finals in Washington three times, placing second twice. During those 12 years he was almost always in the top ribbons and only had about five rails down in his entire career! His winnings (which totalled approximately $65,000 over the years!) would go towards covering the entry fees at the next show. This was the only way I could afford to compete at the A shows.

The two of us were an entertaining duo. My unique equitation style left something to be desired. Pavel would see me warming up in the schooling area and say "Niks, heels down!" Then you'd hear him mutter to himself, "Oh, damn it, just jump the jump." After a couple years of trying he had given up on correcting my poor style.

Striker was a little backyard horse with a crooked blaze among a sea of fancy show horses. Together, we made the perfect odd team. My mother would always say "Striker knows what Nikki wants him to do before she does." This was the secret to our success. We were partners.

Striker jumped with such heart. He always tried his hardest to be clean, even if I placed him wrong to a jump. His show name "Bail Me Out" suited him perfectly. If I missed a distance I could always count on Striker to bail me out! By the time we finished our first round, strangers in the stands would be rooting for us.

I'd prep Striker for a big class by taking him on "happy walks." We had an understanding; I gave him grass and he would bail me out.

During jump offs, my mother would always be at the in gate yelling at the top of her lungs, "go, go, go!" Pat and Pavel would uncontrollably pick up their own feet as Striker sailed over each jump.

My grandmother sat with my grandfather in the stands, and we all joked that she was busy using her mind power to put hexes on the other riders to knock down rails. She would pick a spot to watch from, and if other riders were knocking down rails, she wouldn't move. If no one was knocking down rails, she would move to "a better spot." She was a church going lady, but horse shows brought out her competitive nature!

After Striker did well in a jump-off, my grandmother would quickly run to the warm-up area yelling "my hero!" She was referring to Striker!

My husband Mike, who was my boyfriend through college,

would say there was nothing better than pulling into an A show with a backyard horse, rusty truck and trailer, and taking home a top ribbon.

Red was Striker's favorite color. He seemed to place second at every show. At a show in Northampton, Massachusetts, Striker placed second in the Marshall & Sterling classic. After the show, a cow pinning exhibition event was held. English riders from the show were encouraged to participate and ride the Western horses provided. I knew Striker would enjoy doing something different. I borrowed a Western saddle and entered him in the competition. Striker loved it. He had been turned out with steers on my grandfather's farm, so it was no big deal to him. Riders from earlier that day recognized him and asked, "Isn't that the horse that almost won the Marshall & Sterling classic today?"

Before Mike and I married, my mother explained to him that Striker and horses would always come first for me. She said to him, "If you can accept this, then you would be okay marrying Nikki." She also joked that, "If you can *not* accept this, then you should run the other way while you have a chance."

My dad, Rob Hansen, was so happy that I found "a sucker" as he called it, to help support my expensive hobby. He almost ran from the dinner table to pack up the truck, trailer and horses and ship us off before Mike could change his mind. Lucky for me, Mike didn't change his mind.

The day after we were engaged, I brought Mike to my grandparent's farm to ride and clean stalls. I wanted to see if he really understood what he was in for by marrying a "horse person." Plus, I had a plan. I'd introduce him to riding on Django. Django was my sturdy, 20 year old Welsh Cob pony that I had had since I was six years old. No one could resist Django. The whole family loved him and half the family rode him, from my grandmother to my little cousins. Everybody loved him. He had the personality and smarts of a human, earning him many nicknames. One of them was "Pony Man." My plan worked. I still joke today that

Mike married me because he wanted my pony.

Mike and I were married in September, 2000. After the wedding ceremony in Storrs, Connecticut, we posed for pictures on the horses. I rode Striker and Mike rode Django. I knew then that horses had taken another "sucker" captive into our horse family. Two years later, Pat rode Striker in her wedding and her husband David Towle rode Striker's niece, Sago Lily. When my grandfather passed away in 2006, Striker led the funeral procession as the riderless horse to honor his World War II army service in the last remaining unit of the U.S. Cavalry.

Striker spends his retirement years continuing to spread joy to our family. My husband, mother, friend Bridget and I take him hunter pacing and trail riding regularly. He proved to be a valuable lead horse when I broke my Percheron/Thoroughbred mare, Stormy Sky. Stormy was a rescue horse that was timid about everything around her. She quickly settled down with Striker leading the way on trails. Striker and Stormy love their trips to the beach at Bluff Point in Groton, Connecticut. While Stormy and I swim in the ocean, Mike and Striker sneak off to visit their favorite spot on the beach. They each have their own agenda. Striker is planning to take a sun bath and fall asleep while Mike plans to drink a beer.

My one year old daughter, Julia Marie has been riding Striker from the day she was conceived. I continued to ride him until two days before I went into labor with Julia. I had no doubt that Striker was safe to ride while I was pregnant. Now, Julia rides Striker on my lap with a glow on her face that only another horse person can understand. She giggles when we trot and canter.

Striker has been a "hero," "the little horse," companion and amazing competitor but most importantly, a family member. He has brought joy to four generations of my family. I plan for him to come out of retirement to compete in one more "A" show. This time, Striker's division will be lead-line, with Julia aboard.

⟿ SPIKE

It was Spike or the dog. That was the deal Carole's husband, Bill Smith, had made.

Carole was supposed to be preparing Spike, a six-year-old Quarter Horse who had been raised in Oklahoma, for the annual WYO Quarter Horse Sale. But she had fallen in love with him. Although he wasn't an easy horse, he and Carole had a connection.

Carole had recently lost her beloved Border Collie. She wanted a new dog. Bill didn't much care for dogs. So he came up with an idea.

"You can have Spike if you don't get another dog," Bill told her.

And so the grey Quarter Horse with the snowy mane and tail became Carole's horse. The name Spike originated from the horse's appearance upon his arrival. His bridle path, badly in need of a trim, stood straight up. In addition, the horse had long ears. The name Spike fit.

Spike had been abused and in the process developed a terrible fear of men. If anyone walked into his corral, he would race for the opposite end. Carole worked patiently with him, and in time he began to trust her. But she didn't fool herself. She knew that if she got herself into a tight spot, Spike would look after himself, not her.

Soon Carole and Spike began competing: first in barrel racing and then in pole bending. Spike's athletic ability immediately became apparent. Although he wasn't too fast on the straightaways, he was quick around the poles and barrels. And, despite being a big, stout horse, Spike was light on his feet.

Carole was a seasoned rodeo competitor who had qualified and competed at the National Finals Rodeo prior to owning Spike. She knew rodeos, and rodeo horses. Spike, she says, "has a real rodeo horse mentality. He's tough and competitive with a lot of heart."

Carole wanted to compete more often with Spike, but preparing other horses for the sales kept her busy. So she let her great niece, Jesse, ride him in high school rodeos. Together Jesse and Spike racked up a succession of victories. One of their best events was goat tying, which is in a way, a prelude to calf roping.

Jesse also competed in breakaway roping, a version of calf roping reserved for youngsters. Spike and Jesse tried their hand at team roping as well, serving as both the header (the one who ropes the steer around the horns) and the heeler (the one who ropes the hind feet).

No matter what event Spike competed in, he was always game and willing to try.

When Jesse graduated from high school, Spike returned to Carole. Knowing rodeo as well as she did, Carole was aware of just how much it took out of a horse, especially one like Spike who gave it his all. Spike had worked hard with Jesse, and Carole wanted to be sure he got a break.

However, Spike's driven personality didn't sit well with that idea. He began getting into mischief (something he did throughout his life). Spike had lived for so long at the ranch that he believed he owned it. He would boss the other geldings around and when they were moved from pasture to pasture, he would get out ahead of them and take them on a road trip. He had an unerring sense of exactly where Carole and Bill did not want them to go, and that's just where they would end up.

If Spike was turned out in a pasture up in the hills, he would tear the gate down and come back home, bringing along all the horses who had shared the pasture with him. Spike was also very difficult to catch, so once he got loose on his adventures it was a further adventure rounding him up!

Without the rodeo to occupy him, Spike had become bored. And bored translated into more mischief. Carole knew it was time to find Spike another job.

One of Bill's best friends, Ralph Maynard, had two young grandsons who enjoyed rodeoing. Bill contacted Ralph's daughter, Sharmyn Munoz. He suggested that perhaps Spike might be a good fit for her sons.

At first, Sharmyn wasn't too sure. Spike was a lot of horse, especially for a young boy. Zane was approaching seven; Landon was three years younger. But Zane's barrel horse hadn't proven to be particularly competitive. Zane placed with him, he and the horse did all right, but all right wasn't good enough for Zane. He longed for the thrill of victory, for the opportunity to compete with a horse who wanted it as much as he did.

It didn't take long for Spike to put Sharmyn's mind at ease. The big grey and Zane proved a great match. Suddenly, Zane won everything in sight. In barrel racing the pair was good; in pole bending they were unstoppable. In fact, the first time Zane ran poles with Spike, Spike zipped through them so quickly that Zane fell off. Undeterred, Spike finished the course. And Zane learned to stay on him.

Soon Spike became the talk of New Mexico. Everyone asked, "Where did you get that big, grey horse?" They all wanted to buy him, but Spike was not for sale.

Zane and Spike won every single poles competition they entered together. In fact, Spike's time was often so quick that he and Zane had the fastest time for the entire rodeo, quite an accomplishment for such a young rider. Spike almost never touched a pole during his career, quite an accomplishment for a horse!

In addition to their wins, Zane and Spike earned a lot of great prizes, including saddles.

Spike's love of pranks came to light with his new family as well. He always managed to get out of his pen. Spike enjoyed playing with chains, hooks, bailing wire: anything the silly humans thought could keep him in an enclosure. Once he let himself out he would try to help the other horses escape as well. To Spike, getting loose was like a game he played with the humans to see if he could outsmart them. Usually, he did.

Although Spike could be a bit ornery to work around, Sharmyn never questioned him when Zane climbed aboard. The horse was so well broke and so willing that Zane could do anything with him. Soon Zane began learning to rope on him, and he and Spike competed in some breakaway roping events.

With all of his success on Spike, Zane's confidence received a huge boost. And Spike found himself a member of the family. Sharmyn says, "If I was ever going to clone a horse, it would have been Spike."

Carole gave Spike, a tough horse with a tough start in life, a second chance. In return, Spike gave several families the thrill of victory, and the joy of working with a talented and willing athlete who gave it all he had. Carole says, "Even when he was 20 he was totally sound and showed no sign of stiffness. He just kept going as hard as he could."

Yet with all of his willingness to compete and be part of a team, Spike always remained an individual, with a unique and mischievous personality.

Carole may have other dogs, but she will never have another Spike. Regarding the deal she made with Bill, she says, "I'm glad I did it!" There is no doubt in anyone's mind that she made the right decision.

AND MORE

⟿ Don't Know Much About Geometry

As a student, math was Mary Ellen Berish's worst subject. And geometry was harder than any other math, more difficult than any other subject. She hated all those figures, those angles, hated them with a passion.

Still, Mary Ellen was attending school in Millbrook, New York, and she knew she would have to pass the Regents exam. So she got extra help from one of the nuns, working on her theorems, learning about circles and angles and parallel lines. She passed her geometry class, passed her Regents exam. She slammed the book on geometry. She was done; she would never have to deal with this again!

How was she to know that later on in life all those figures would prove so important to her?

Years later, Mary Ellen, now McDonald, with a young daughter and a son on the way, found herself watching something that transformed her life. Her new home in Wellington, Florida was a horseman's paradise. Mary Ellen had always ridden; horses were a big part of her life. She had learned to jump, and competed in lower level events. But what she was watching was different, something out of another universe.

A young man sat elegantly on a regal horse, dancing around the arena in sublime harmony. The horse appeared to perform of his own accord, with no obvious requests from his partner. The performance was beautiful and so well done that it looked easy.

It was Mary Ellen's first glimpse of upper level dressage, and it seized her with a desire to ride like the young man was riding.

She plunged into dressage with a passion, and soon found herself an excellent coach, Ruth Hogan-Paulsen.

But Ruth's description of dressage gave Mary Ellen cause for alarm. "Dressage," said Ruth, "is all about geometry." The circles, the lines, the angles, the precision, were all a reflection of that hated childhood subject.

Now the things that Mary Ellen hated most in life have become what she loves the most. She works hard to perfect her circles and her diagonals, to get her lines straight and her angles correct. There is, she says, "something magical about the horse that it can make that happen, that it can take something so boring and make it fascinating."

And the rider that turned Mary Ellen's life around? Although she was unaware of who he was at that first eye opening glimpse, she later found out his name. It was Robert Dover.

⟿ Riding Off Into The Sunset

Many of us dreamed, as children, of owning our own ponies and spending our days with them in complete freedom: exploring woods and fields, swimming with our mounts, and playing cowboys and Indians. Although most of us never got to live that dream, here's the story of one little girl who did.

All Elizabeth Garrett wanted to do was ride. As a three-year-old, there were no horses or ponies available to her, so Elizabeth was forced to get creative. Her mom's sewing machine, encased in a hard cover, was similar in shape to a horse's back. So ride she did, on a sewing machine.

Luckily, she didn't have to pretend for long. Her dad took pity on his daughter, buying her a Shetland pony named Sugar. Sugar, however, was anything but sweet. Instead, she was a typical pony.

The family lived in the sleepy southern town of Madison, Mississippi, not far from Jackson. Madison's dusty streets still featured hitching rails gracing the fronts of some of the stores. Sugar, along with Wilbureen, the big brown pig Elizabeth's dad had bought her, made their home at The Strawberry Patch. In a former lifetime the land had been just that. It had since become "16th Section Land," land deeded by the government for use as a working farm, or school land.

In addition to boarding stables, The Strawberry Patch featured a pond graced by the two white geese Quacker and Buttons, and an antebellum home turned country store, Elizabeth's favorite place.

The sight and scent of string licorice hanging in loops from the rafters greeted Elizabeth as she entered the store. Inside she would find an exciting array of penny candy, Moon Pies, and giant dill pickles in big wooden barrels. Out on the back porch a 10-cent Coca Cola machine waited to soothe parched throats with its refreshing beverage.

The Coke machine proved to be one of Elizabeth's favorite attractions in the store. After purchasing a beverage from the machine, and pulling the frosty bottle out from its metal slats, Elizabeth and her friends would jump off the porch onto their ponies' backs and head out to ride the endless acres of fields and trails that circled the town. One of her friend's ponies enjoyed ice cold Cokes right out of the bottle.

The best time of year was Christmas, when festive trees located throughout the store were decorated with unique and whimsical ornaments. It was a family tradition to buy a new ornament from these trees each year to add to their own collection.

Elizabeth had inherited the horse gene from someone, and it turned out it came from her father. Deciding that it would be fun to join Elizabeth on her rides, her father bought a saddle horse named Sunny, a sorrel with a blaze face and stockings. On weekends, the two of them would ride together when her father got home after work.

The best part of the ride always came on the way home. As they headed back to the barn with the sun setting, Elizabeth and her father would hold hands and ride into the sunset, pretending that they were riding to Tucson. Although Elizabeth isn't sure why they chose Tucson, it stemmed in part from their mutual love of the West.

Intrigued by the joy Elizabeth and her father found in horses and riding, Elizabeth's brother Jay decided that he, too, wanted to join in the fun and hopped up on Sugar one day. It was a short lived decision. Ray Zirker, who owned Strawberry Patch, drove by in his white convertible, wearing a big sombrero. The sight sent Sugar flying, dumping Elizabeth's brother, and then dragging him. That proved the end of his equestrian career.

As Elizabeth outgrew Sugar, more horses were added to the farm: Velvet, a Morgan that the family rescued; Dutchess, a strawberry roan; and Golden Girl. Since her Dad worked for the Illinois Central and Gulf Railroad, feeding the horses was never a challenge. The railroad hauled a lot of freight, and much of that freight was grain. Often the grain bags would erupt, resulting in spillage. It never went to waste. Her dad had his men gather it up in burlap bags for feed for the horses.

Dutchess soon added to the herd herself, surprising everyone with a filly which Elizabeth's mom named Snap Shot. No one had known Dutchess was pregnant when she was purchased. Dutchess surprised everyone once again when she proved she had tremendous talent for jumping. In order to wean Snap Shot, the family had moved her. To get back to her foal, Dutchess cleared a massive gate. Her ability to jump fences might also explain how she became pregnant without anyone's knowledge!

Life in a sleepy southern town, though idyllic to Elizabeth and her friends, sometimes was just not quite enough for their equine buddies. They longed for the spotlight—and theygot it. Sunny made an appearance in a Sunbeam™ bread commercial. Velvet got more than her share of the spotlight: she was on the cover of MS magazine (with beautiful Mona Britt dipping her toe in the water from her back) and took part in the Dixie National Parade; in addition Velvet posed in a commercial with Elizabeth's mom astride in a white dress.

As the herd grew, Elizabeth's father moved them to a 250 acre farm. Board there would hardly break the bank. Five, yes, five dollars a month for grazing rights. The farm was owned by the Minigers, immigrants from Germany who raised corn, cows, and soybeans.

Life continued to grow sweeter for Elizabeth. In the morning, her parents would drop her off at the farm. All day long she'd ride with the owners' daughters, Lou Ann and Marietta. Sometimes she rode bareback; sometimes it was western. One year she received a green bareback pad as a gift. Just as the sewing machine cover had one day served as her horse, the green bareback pad became her "English" saddle.

Riding was pure play for Elizabeth; the freedom was exhilarating. All day she and her friends would explore the dirt roads and territory surrounding their homes. They played cowboys and Indians, jumped across streams on their ponies, and swam them in the pond.

On shortcuts into town, narrow dirt roads, they would stop and pluck some ears of corn, shucking them, and feed the husks to the horses. It didn't matter that they had no knives to split the watermelons growing nearby on the vines. Smashing them on the ground worked just fine, and the luscious interior could be shared with their mounts.

When the "horse shows" (which were more like rodeos), were in town, they would ride in to watch them. Lunch came with them on their adventures, generally a peanut butter sandwich and a coke.

One Christmas Elizabeth went to the barn and discovered a new pony in a stall. He wore a red bow and on the stall was a wood burned sign her parents had made. It read: "Elizabeth's Peppy." The Welsh pony was Elizabeth's Christmas gift. That was one of the best Christmases!

These idyllic years of childhood ended when Elizabeth went off to college. It was, Elizabeth says, "the best childhood of anyone I know."

But leaving her childhood behind wasn't all bad. All those years of riding off into the sunset holding hands with her Dad on the way to Tucson had created their own happy ending. On a blind date arranged by friends, Elizabeth met Greg Garrett. They've been together ever since.

In the end Elizabeth did ride off into the sunset—with a guy from Tucson.

⤳ TIP
By Crissy Hewitt

When I was 12, my mom promised that we could buy a horse for me. I had been riding and showing her young palomino Quarter Horse, Dolly, who was an amazingly quiet and tolerant horse who obediently jumped when directed toward an obstacle. I learned about pacing, rhythm, and the virtue of being calm while on course from Dolly. However, my legs were getting longer and Dolly was a mere 14.3 hands.

So, along with my mom and trainer Cheryl Bailey, we went "horse shopping." Mom wanted a palomino so "we could ride in town parades together and our horses would match." I nodded but vowed to myself never to be seen riding in a parade: way too silly and childish for a grown up twelve-year-old.

We had just about given up finding a palomino English hunter. Then we received a phone call from Janet Lawson, a Quarter Horse judge and a friend of Cheryl's. She knew of a six-year-old palomino gelding. He was a Quarter Horse/Thoroughbred cross. Formerly a stud, he had been gelded and purchased by a couple in Southbury, Connecticut. The wife wanted a western pleasure gelding that was flashy enough for the show ring but quiet enough for the trails.

Mom, Cheryl, and I drove down to have a look. On the way, Cheryl made a point of mentioning that she had, in fact, already been there to give the gelding a test ride. He had dumped her over a six-inch crossrail.

"Not exactly the best first impression," she said. However, he was big boned, beautiful, and had a naturally balanced canter.

We pulled into the dusty driveway and were met by a large, portly man who introduced himself as the owner. Standing there at a gate by the barn was a skinny, golden Thoroughbred. He stomped his feet incessantly at the black flies and looked on with suspicious curiosity.

The owner's wife came wobbling down to the barn. I'll never forget it: in heels and a large black and white polka-dotted dress. I was sure she wouldn't be introducing us to the gelding for sale. Much to my surprise, she mumbled a meek "hello" and walked past us, grabbing a lead rope on the way.

At the gate the young gelding nickered in anticipation of what was to come, or perhaps at the prospect of escaping the black flies. I immediately noticed the poor quality of the horse's feet: the front right, flat and pancaked; and the front left, shod so poorly it looked nearly like a club foot. Still, there was something intriguing about the skinny horse.

"This is Brandon," said the woman. "He's really a big sweetheart." Something in her voice told me she had experienced a quality other than sweet from this horse.

We agreed that she would ride him first and then I would be allowed a test ride. A giant western saddle was flung onto his bony back and his feet were hastily picked out. I looked on, taking it all in. The horse had giant, beautiful brown eyes that looked on with a certain kind of wily spunk. Yet at the same time, he looked unsure and mistrustful.

With her western bridle slung around one arm, the owner reached with the other to pull off his halter. At that moment, the gelding flipped his head up, nearly brushing the ceiling with his muzzle, and lifted the poor woman right off of her feet. As she regained her balance, he pushed past the husband and veered into an unoccupied stall. My mother sighed, demonstrating her uncertainty about my riding this clearly unruly beast.

Nevertheless, twenty minutes later, I was trotting him around the dusty ring. The first thing I noticed once I was on his back were the curved, unique tips of his ears. He had small, elegant ears that flicked back and forth with uncertainty and the tip of each ear was indescribably adorable and perfect.

Brandon was lazy and shuffled, rather than trotted. Cheryl let me canter a few strides and I was in love. His canter was a long, slow lope that would put you to sleep: that is, until he spooked at something. I could tell he was capable of moving quickly if something inspired him to do so.

Although my mother was still unsure about the purchase, not a week later Brandon (later to be named Tip because of those beautiful ears) was bumping along in the back of our stock trailer to his new home. That was in the fall of 1997.

Tip spent the winter munching on hay with his new pasture mate, Dolly. Without an indoor, we couldn't do much but feed and muck all winter long. In the spring, to say that we had a very different horse from the one that we bought the previous fall would be an understatement. Tip was wild, like a horse that had never been backed. At times I could barely lead him. He would stand and strike at what seemed like imaginary objects.   I was determined not to let him get the best of me, but my mother was not so sure. After I had fallen off a few times and Tip had struck out at one of us while we were mucking or feeding, mom called a few dealers to come and look at him. I was frustrated and felt powerless. I had stopped riding him, partly because of fear and partly because I was afraid of failure.

Then, one day after school, I made my decision. I knew this horse was special. He had personality, he had spunk, and somehow we had made an odd connection. Even if he was disobedient, unruly, and, at times, dangerous, there was something about him. So I came home from school, had a discussion with him, put the tack on, and off we went into the woods. From that day on I was determined, and while every day after was definitely not perfect, I knew that it would work out. And, for the most part, it did.

That summer we worked on opening his stride to help him use his back and hindquarters properly. He started to learn his leads, and we worked him through poles. Why I ever thought Tip would learn to jump is still a mystery to me. I had never met such an uncoordinated, clumsy, and disinterested horse when it came to obstacles. He would trot at the poles and either trip over each one or jump the entire lot of them.

Finally though, he started to learn and he did get better. With his improved nutrition and workout regime, his long, scrawny body became muscled and powerful. Even the structure of his feet improved with the excellent shoeing of Tim Kriz.

Years went by and I started showing Tip. Our first mark of success was when he began jumping all of the jumps in the course without a refusal. Once we mastered that, next up was jumping all of the jumps in the correct order. Finally, we got to jumping all the jumps in order and on the correct leads. His beautiful style soon brought us many ribbons in the hunter ring.

For summer after summer, every Sunday morning before the sun came up, I would venture to the barn to see the damage Tip had done to his braids. We would spend hours Saturday nights putting them in (no less than 33 braids was standard for his long, cresty neck and thick white mane).

In January 2001, Tip sustained a catastrophic injury from a tangle with a gate and nearly died. He separated his right leg from his chest cavity, ripping his pectoral muscle clean apart from his body. After four hours of surgery, 200 stitches and six staple guns, he spent over a month tied on cross ties, where he was not allowed to move. One hundred and nine days after the injury, I was back on, walking him every day, building his strength again.

While many vets said he would never be more than a pasture ornament, it was only soft tissue damage. He avoided infection and healed beautifully. He is just as sound today as he was before that injury. His incredible recovery is no doubt largely due to the veterinary expertise and devotion of a great friend and vet, Dr. Michelle Ferraro of Millbrook Equine Veterinary Clinic.

As a senior in high school, I worked for and rode with Leslie and Reinhart Teetor in Pine Plains, New York. Tip went to spend the spring months there in preparation for the summer show season. He wasn't used to staying in a stall for more than the time it took him to eat his meals so this new lifestyle was a challenge for Tip, considering his energy level. As a result, he was always looking for something to play with.

One day, a fellow boarder and great friend, Karen Manning, went to the paddock to bring Tip in. His chain shank was nowhere in sight. Just as she turned to go back to the barn for another, she caught a glimpse of the rope hanging high from a nearby tree. This was the beginning of Tip's fixation with and need for toys. To prevent boredom, he would play with almost anything that he could get his hooves or teeth around.

When Tip returned home, I had begun a project building some jumps and repairing rails of the ring fence. The new boards I had purchased were stacked neatly just on the outside of the paddock. Each day, when I went to the pile for a board, it seemed the pile was even smaller than I had remembered it to be. Then one sunny afternoon I discovered the culprit. Coming out onto our back porch, I saw Tip rearing and squealing at the far corner of the field with a two-by-four in his mouth. Later that day, I circled the four-acre paddock collecting stolen, chewed on two-by-fours.

In the spring of 2002, I graduated from Housatonic Valley Regional High School and planned my departure for Mount Holyoke College the following fall. Due to a very generous sponsor, Tip had a stall at the large, sophisticated Equestrian Center right on campus. While I was nervous about Tip's transition to a big barn with very little turnout, it beat the alternative of leaving him home. That was something I never would have done.

He had developed a strong attachment to me and depended on me to show him the way. As such, at MHC, Tip waited for me to come in the afternoons after class to take him riding.

I would walk into the sixty-five stall barn and greet fellow riders, barn staff, and other horses nearby. Tip, upon hearing my voice in the barn, would whinny to hurry my arrival to his stall. His voice flooded the aisles of the barn each time that I arrived to take him on an adventure.

And that is what we had: adventures. We were good and worked in the ring on dressage or jumping, but we also took off into the woods on long walks. Or we went to the cross-country field where I dozed, draped backwards over Tip's rump, as he grazed.

Our adventures were all good distractions as long as I was there to take part. When I was at class, however, or held up with homework, Tip looked for other ways to entertain himself.

He went through pasture mates quickly because he would shred their blankets and the owners sought less destructive playmates for their horses. Then, he decided his paddock was boring or not big enough so he began yanking boards off of the fencing. After escaping twice through this method of fence dismantling, the barn management informed me that Tip would not be welcome to partake in turnout at all if he couldn't remain in the fence. I suggested toys, since I knew that might entertain him.

Tip became quite the spectacle. His paddock contained plastic garbage can tops, which he flung like a Frisbee; rags, which he whipped back and forth with his teeth; broom stick handles, which were good for chewing on, and finally his favorite, an old hose. I knew the hose would work best because he had reached through the fence at home and run away with our hose on more than one occasion. Nearby horses stood and watched curiously at the sight of a large palomino rearing and jumping while swinging a wildly flying hose.

The toys worked. They distracted Tip from dismantling the fence and escaping. Tip's turnout privileges were not revoked.

In his stall, he continued his bizarre antics. It was almost as if his play time in the paddock helped him to develop unconventional habits. The barn purchased their sawdust in bulk and occasionally a large block of whole wood appeared in the shavings. If Tip found one in his stall, he would grasp it with his teeth and drop it in his feed bucket. One day I asked a barn hand why there were three pieces of wood in Tip's bucket. I thought that she may have put them there knowing Tip's interest in playing with odd toys. No person had put the wood in Tip's bucket: he had.

Tip also had an old, cut-off hose in his stall which he played with on a regular basis. Each stall had a hay hole in the ceiling so that barn staff could throw hay in from the loft above. One morning, a barn hand reported that she found Tip's hose on the loft floor, not far from the hay hole above his stall. Exactly how Tip was able to get his hose flung up through the hay hole is a mystery, but by that time no one believed him incapable of such a stunt.

It wasn't until a light bulb, protected by a safety grill, was shattered one night that Tip lost his hose privilege. Although the light bulb was in an aisle by at least six other stalls, there was only one possible culprit: one horse that had a weapon to whip through the stall bars and shatter the bulb.

Tip's antics continued until the end of his MHC career and beyond when he returned home to Falls Village. He is nearly 19 years old, yet he continues to be opinionated. He still bucks and squeals in the field for no reason, rolls goofily down the snowy hillside, and in general continues to entertain viewers.

Despite many a fall, a broken ankle, and a few stitches, I would say that he has been the best experience of my life.

⤳ Faith Brings Extreme Makeover: Home Edition to Freedom Hills

They call it Freedom Hills Therapeutic Riding Program, for it gives people freedom from wheelchairs and crutches. Those who are physically challenged may be unable to go on nature walks on their own feet, but sitting on the back of a horse gives them four strong legs to take them into the woods and trails and places they could not normally go. Renee Luther has been running Freedom Hills in Port Deposit, Maryland, for 26 years. She does it out of love and "for the hugs and smiles."

However, life at Freedom Hills had become a serious struggle. Renee's husband Carl had recently died from liver cancer. Overburdened by the physical demands of her job and handicapped by the physical plant they were working out of, the Luther family needed help. Renee's ability to reach the number of people she would like to help was compromised by her tiny indoor arena (she described it as "a glorified 20 meter circle"), and her small, inadequate barn. It was so drafty that "you were always in the wind even when you came out of it." The support poles for the roof had to be surrounded by pylons so the students didn't hit their knees on them.

Renee's house was not wheelchair accessible, and it was so poorly built that the windows would blow out when the winds picked up. The list of problems with the house went on and on:

inadequate insulation, electrical problems, mold, and front steps so rickety that someone could easily have broken a leg on them. The stove lacked an oven and had only one working burner (Renee did a lot of the cooking on the wood stove), and the air conditioner hadn't worked for three years.

On top of that, Renee and her two children were living in the house in which Carl, their husband and father, had died. Renee had attempted CPR, which failed to rouse him. The devastating memories continued to haunt her and the children. What were they going to do?

Renee had grown up surrounded by foster children that her mother, Rosemarie Sherrard-Linton, took in and raised. When one was hurt and had to go the hospital, Renee met the occupational therapist. Instantly impressed, Renee thought, "wow, what a job, helping little children!"

Her dad, Holmes Sherrard, had been an avid horseback rider, and purchased the farm when Renee was just two years old. He died when she was six, leaving her mom with a 156 acre farm. Her mom didn't let that stop her. She paid off the farm by the time Renee was 15.

Rosemarie had met a wonderful new man when Renee was 13, who soon became another dad to her. Yet Rosemarie was determined to pay off the farm on her own. Once that was done, she married the new man: Howard Linton (known as "Buddy" or "Dad" to most people).

This determination and drive passed directly down to Renee.

A few horses lived on the farm, and when Renee was 10, she'd started showing them. While initially she competed in gymkhanas, she later veered towards the English disciplines, settling on jumpers, dressage, and finally, eventing. Attending Centenary College in New Jersey, Renee majored in Equine Studies and minored in recreational therapy.

During college, she spent three years interning at Somerset Hills for the Handicapped in Bedminster, New Jersey, training under Octavio Brown, one of the most distinguished riding-for-the-handicapped instructors in the nation as well as a many-time president of the North American Riding for the Handicapped Association.

All this prepared Renee exquisitely for her mission in life. She returned home to the farm. With her love of horses and of helping people, starting a therapeutic riding program of her own was the only way to go. She began gathering some suitable ponies, and soon she had her very first student, Mark, a little boy with muscular dystrophy. Mark was a son of one of Renee's teachers.

Soon Renee's plate looked like one of a teenager at an all-you-can-eat buffet. She taught up to 50 lessons a week to physically, mentally, and emotionally challenged students, organized the fundraising efforts necessary to keep Freedom Hills running, ran a lesson program for able-bodied students, and managed the daily care for the 26 horses at the farm while home schooling daughter Ellie and son Alex. In addition, she had worked hard to obtain her Advanced Instructors Certification with NARHA, her Level Three in Centered Riding, her Level Two in Parelli Natural Horsemanship and her Advanced Certification with the American Riding Instructors Certification Program.

It was at this point in her over the top life that Carl died. Although Renee felt overwhelmed at times, she kept her focus on the Lord and immediately looked to Him for help. One of her favorite verses starts with "Philippians 4:3 Rejoice in the Lord always and again I say Rejoice. Be anxious for nothing but in all things through prayer and supplication let your requests be known unto God. Then the peace of God which passes all understanding will guard your heart and your mind through Christ Jesus." Renee would find herself repeating these verses daily.

The Luther family loved the television show Extreme

Makeover: Home Edition. In fact it was their favorite show. They would all gather to watch it, to feel the joy of watching other families have their lives dramatically improved.

Extreme Makeover: Home Edition had developed an Extreme Plan: they would help one family in each state over the next two years. As they considered Maryland, they came to a decision. For this area so rich in horses and equestrian history, they would choose a therapeutic riding stable.

Most families (or their friends or relatives) sent out videos to Extreme Makeover, hoping to be chosen for a new home. Although the Luther family desperately needed a new facility, they didn't make a video. They didn't have time. With a 156 acre farm to run, with 26 horses to care for and lessons to teach, there were never enough hours in the day.

But they wanted to be part of the show, wanted a new facility that would help them to help others. And Renee had a secret weapon: her faith. Wanting an indoor and new barn so much, she knew it would come. She just didn't know through what avenue it would arrive. She never contacted the show. God did the work for her. Extreme Makeover: Home Edition contacted Renee and Freedom Hills. Fifty e-mails were sent to horse facilities in Maryland: Freedom Hills was one of them.

At first, Renee didn't believe it. Returning home from the Pony Club Nationals in Kentucky in July (daughter Ellie had qualified and done quite well) Renee was met by Freedom Hill's Program Assistant, Lynne Henderson.

"Have you checked your e-mail?" she asked.

"Come on Lynne, it's summer. I don't have time for e-mail!" was Renee's reply.

"Extreme Makeover has contacted you about doing a build."

"No way," said Renee. "You're kidding." Renee worked from 7 a.m. to 10 p.m.: she was exhausted and in no mood for pranks. But Lynne insisted that she check her e-mail. And there it was: a message from JD Myers of Extreme Makeover: Home Edition.

Renee poured out her whole story to JD: the death of her husband, the tiny indoor riding ring and old barn, the house and all its problems. JD called her, and they subsequently talked many times at length. Then he told Renee, "I will come out and do your video."

He promised to call over the weekend to let her know when they would come. When Renee didn't hear anything, she thought, "Oh well, I have been disappointed before." But at 11 p.m. Sunday evening, the phone rang. It was JD. He told her he would be coming out on Wednesday.

Renee was instantly energized by the call. She and her volunteers began frantically cleaning, getting ready for the visit.

A camera team came to the farm and shadowed Renee, following her around all day as she cared for the horses, ran the farm, and taught the lessons. JD interviewed Renee, as well as other people at the barn.

Then the suspense began, along with some interesting twists along the way. JD would call her regularly with more questions. Then there would be silence. Nothing.

Ellie, Alex, and Renee made plans to attend a heavy metal Christian concert, featuring a band named Purple Door. In anticipation of the concert, Ellie streaked her hair pink. Renee thought it looked really cute.

This prompted a phone call a few days later from JD. They needed more footage for the video. JD's boss, Quentin, would be out in two days.

An emergency bleaching session took place, changing Ellie's pink hair to the palest of blondes.

Then Quentin came out for a two-hour visit. He stayed for six. More phone calls followed; more photos and video were shot.

At one point, Renee asked, "How do people find out if

they've lost?"

JD answered, "People just figure it out."

Renee asked, "Well, could you just drop me a note that says "loser?"

Instead, JD said, "Because we share the same faith, I will call you."

On September 12th, Renee was at Denny's grabbing a meal after church with her friend Tina when her phone rang. It was JD. His voice sounded sad as he said, "I just called to tell you."

"Oh no," thought Renee, "I have lost."

Then the voice changed, "You're in the top five!" JD yelled.

Renee started screaming, "Tina, Tina, we're in the top five!" Luckily, the Denny's wasn't particularly crowded.

JD went on to tell Renee that their door-knock day, the day that Ty would show up with his bullhorn were she to win, would be October 14th at 8 a.m.

So the roller-coaster ride continued. Some days Renee was sure they had won and Ty Pennington would be in her front yard. Other days she was equally positive that she had lost. But, as with all things, Renee relied on her faith and the Word of God to see her through. When people would say "if you win" Renee would say "Oh no, it is not if we win, it is when we win." Yet, she was sure the other four families were praying just as hard as the Luthers were.

If the bus should show up, Renee felt, then that was the avenue the Lord wanted the family to use to get a new house and indoor. If it didn't show up, then the Lord had another plan. Renee prayed for the other four families to win as well as her own family.

One of the challenges unique to the Luther family was that, were they chosen, they would need to find homes for all of their 26 horses while the barn was being refurbished. This would include her favorite horse Giver (Abundantly Giving). He was

Renee's own horse. He was born on the farm, with Renee assisting at his birth. She'd trained him herself. He was so well schooled that she was able to jump around the novice level eventing course at Fair Hill with nothing but a Parelli halter.

When Ellie started proving her talent as a rider, Renee couldn't afford to buy her the nice horse she needed, and ended up giving her Giver. But the Lord eventually blessed Renee with another special horse, an off-the-track Thoroughbred named Carousel for which she paid $500.

All these horses would have to find temporary homes, and in addition to that challenge, they would have only an hour to get everybody moved! The producers wanted to make the horses leaving the farm a part of the show, so Renee could not move them herself. She needed to find five volunteers to help her.

The help came to Renee from several sources. A good friend, Pam Butkewitz, volunteered to oversee the moving of the horses. Hilltop Farm, a top-of-the-line sporthorse facility located nearby in Colora, Maryland, offered to provide homes for 12 of the horses. The other horses would go to LG Equestrian Center, Lee Reynolds, Irish Tulip Farm, and Patty Fry.

There was so much to do. Trailers had to be arranged; packets of food, supplements, and medications needed to be put together. Hay would have to be loaded. And some of the horses were "special needs" horses—ones with medical problems or age related infirmities that required specific care.

As the morning of October 14th dawned, the family was sitting around their family room talking about horses and soccer. Renee, surprisingly, displayed no trace of nervousness. Instead she felt relaxed and peaceful. If the bus showed up, it would be awesome. However, if it didn't arrive, that would be fine because she knew their needs would come to them one way or another.

And then they heard it. "Good morning Luther family!"

Renee could hardly believe it. The relaxed woman was gone: in her place was a wild woman! Renee remembers feeling as though she were having an out of body experience. Ty Pennington was there, in her front yard!

Renee ran into his arms. She could barely breathe.

"Are you all right?" he asked. "You've been through so much, how have you done it? And despite all you've been through, you've dedicated your lives to helping others."

While trying to catch her breath, Renee answered that she was a Philippians 4 kind of woman. She recited to Ty the wonderful Philippians 4:3 verse which she had repeated to herself over and over throughout all of her trials.

It seemed impossible that it could get any better than it already was, knowing that the farm and house would have a complete makeover, that clients would be able to be served comfortably throughout the winter, and more clients would be able to come. Yet there was more.

The Luthers were going to Italy! Accompanying them would be two Disney executives: Kevin Young and Keith Pagan, who were already scoping out the country for the best spots to take the Luthers. Italy was truly a godsend.

In 2006 the Luther family, including Carl, had scraped the money together to do a Mission trip to Egypt. They ministered at an orphanage in a place called "Garbage City." Renee had asked the travel agent if they could get a long layover somewhere. Money was always tight so she thought it would be great to see more of the world without paying more money. The layover the agent arranged was an overnight in Rome.

How awesome it was, thought Renee, that the Lord, through Disney Adventures, sent Renee, Ellie, and Alex back to Italy. They'd known they wanted to go back—and now they were! Part of their fascination with the area was their love for ancient history. This time they spent two nights in Rome, one night in Florence, and two nights in Venice.

It took a week to rebuild the Luther family home, stable,

and indoor ring. Fifteen hundred tradespeople and volunteers contributed their efforts to making a new life for a family that did so much for others. Renee's sister Robyn helped out, something she has done throughout the years, and which Renee greatly appreciates. Even the mayor of the town came out to pitch in, cleaning and vacuuming the new home.

When they arrived home, they could barely contain themselves. What would their new home and barn look like? Then they were looking at the bus and the five thousand spectators who had turned out to watch, cheer them on, and scream, "Move That Bus!" And, "Move That Trailer!" for a trailer had been placed in front of the barn to screen it.

What they saw, says Renee, was "a castle! It's just amazing to know that we are living in a castle." (Photos of the amazing new house can be viewed at www.ctextremedream.com). The designers and crew "absolutely nailed" the family's personality in their choice of interior design and furniture. It's so comfortable that as soon as they walked in the door the Luthers felt right at home. And Renee adds, "When you sit on the couches, it feels like they give you a hug." The house is "not like a museum; it's us."

Ellie, who loves music, felt it was cool that Paige (one of Extreme Makeover's designers) designed the "pretty" metal room for her. And Alex loves his room so much, with his flight simulator, that he gave Rib, the designer, an "A"!

The whole downstairs is wheelchair accessible, something the family really wanted so they could have everybody over and have lots of get-togethers. The new barn and indoor were very exciting to Renee because she knew her students would be able to ride all winter in comfort. It is state-of-the-art with great footing and an insulated ceiling to help keep out the cold.

Riders, staff, and horses are all now "so much more comfortable." The barn houses 19 stalls (previously there were 14), two wash stalls, and a beautiful, well designed, tack room.

Renee reports that in addition to the fabulous facility the

Luthers received, the awareness of the community has become much greater. Some wonderful school horses have been donated, including an adorable Welsh pony and a Third Level Hanoverian dressage horse. Both the number of students and volunteers have increased.

"It's a dream come true," she says. "We can serve more people, ride year round, touch a lot more lives."

Renee has been introduced to new programs sponsored by the county, including one that taught her how to better manage her pastures.

She can't speak highly enough about her builder Clark Turner (Clark Turner Signature Homes) who was "absolutely wonderful," and Steven and Kim Risk from Paul Risk Associates, who built the barn.

Clark's company continues to help her, always being "right there" should anything need to be fixed. And he has plenty to say about the experience of doing Extreme Makeover. "It was the most rewarding week of my life. I'm so proud of my workers and how much they gave of themselves to help others."

Ty himself said "Horses are your life—they are what puts the smiles on the kid's faces." By doing the makeover, "it's almost as if Freedom Hills has gotten that smile and hug itself."

In addition to being the biggest build Extreme Makeover had ever done (between the house, indoor, and barn refurbishment), the whole thing happened amazingly fast. The Luthers were contacted in July; the makeover took place a few short months later, in October.

When the show aired, the Luthers discovered there was yet another surprise in store for them. Baltimore Hyundai dealers got together and gave them a Santa Fe, a seven passenger SUV. Renee says "not only do we live in a mansion, but we have been blessed in so many ways."

Looking back at the whole experience, Renee declares, "It is amazing what the Lord has done."

⁓ꝰTHE HORSE

"The Horse," an exhibit organized by the American Museum of Natural History, presents an amazing overview of the way horses have influenced our lives. Today there are an estimated 58.5 million horses in the world.

"From its origins more than 50 million years ago, through its relationship with humans over the millennia, to its roles in modern society, the horse has left an indelible mark on our world," says Sandra Olsen, co-creator of the exhibit.

Samuel Taylor, director of the Carnegie Museum (Philadelphia, Pennsylvania), says the exhibit offers "an in-depth look at how every facet of human existence has been influenced by our relationship with the horse."

Ross MacPhee, co-curator of "The Horse," says, "Puny but clever, enterprising humans needed an animate energy source that was both mobile and controllable—hence the domestic horse. What no one could have foreseen was that, over the millennia, while we molded the horse to our ends, the horse also molded us by changing the scale and scope of what could be carried, traded, fought over, or used to make life better—in short, civilization as we know it."

One of the exhibit's six parts, "The Nature of Horses," looks at the many extraordinary qualities of horses that have made them so important and useful to humans. "Their bodies are powerful, living machines that can work all day powered only by grass, while they have both the ability to comprehend subtle commands and the motivation to obey them. Horses accept the authority of herd leaders. which makes them receptive to taking orders."

"How We Shaped Horses, How Horses Shaped Us," looks at how horses and humans have influenced each other. Humans have remade horses, creating dozens of breeds in search of faster, stronger, bigger, or smaller equines. At the same time, horses have changed the way we travel, fight wars, work, and play.

Men on horseback or in horse-drawn chariots were the ultimate weapon for thousands of years. From chariots, to European knights of the Middle Ages, to Genghis Khan's Mongolian army, the samurai of Japan, and the Spanish conquistadors, horses have been the foundation for conducting war in societies around the world.

Horses in the nineteenth century helped Europe and the Americas enter the Industrial Age by pulling carriages, fire engines, and carts on streets; delivering milk, ice, and coal; towing barges along canals, and herding cattle across the North American plains.

On nearly every continent horses have served as symbols of power, nobility, and wealth. They have even been considered gods in some cultures.

For most of human history, the fastest means of land transportation has been by horseback. Our legendary Pony Express, created in 1860, reduced the amount of time it took to get a letter across the United States from 25 days by carriage to ten by horseback.

Horses are one of the world's fastest land animals. We constantly test these magnificent athletes for speed and agility in their role as our athletic partners.

The horse's role has shifted over time: away from warfare, travel, and work, to recreation and companionship.

No matter what aspect of our lives we consider, the horse has had an influence. How has the horse affected your life?

ANN JAMIESON

Ann Jamieson is a United States Equestrian Federation judge licensed in hunters, jumpers, and hunt seat equitation. She shows her own horse, Fred Astaire, in hunters and First Level Dressage, in addition she has recently taken up the sport of reining.

Ann has written numerous articles for magazines and newspapers. She currently writes for "Today's Equestrian" magazine.

This is Ann's third volume of "For the Love of the Horse."

Ann lives in Kent, Connecticut, with her Ocicat Hobbes and Bombay cat Isabelle.